The Innovation Animals

The Innovation Animals

For -

Dad, who got me into Bradbury and Tolkien

Mom, who covered the bases with Humpty Dumpty and Seuss

Elizabeth, who pushed Parker and Sedaris ... worked for me!

Danika, Kurt and Drew, who for years put up with such poorly voice-acted Sendak, Silverstein and Rowling.

Praise for the Innovation Animals

"Not many business books can claim to be beautiful as well as useful, but THE INNOVATION ANIMALS fills the bill. The ABC's of innovation are richly conveyed via attractive illustrations, entertaining anecdotes, and poems. Yes, poems. Read it for yourself, then pass it along to your creative friends."

— **Daniel H. Pink**, author of **DRIVE** and **TO SELL IS HUMAN**

"Each of us has the capacity to be an innovator. INNOVATION ANIMALS ignites that internal innovation spark, showcasing important attributes made memorable by the pairing with respective innovation animals, and supported by best practice stories to bring the attributes and capacity for innovation to life. A charming, insightful and highly pragmatic source of inspiration for any reader."

— **Brad Smith, President & Chief Executive Officer, Intuit**
(ranked by Forbes as the #3 Greatest Business Leader alive today)

"True to form, Jeff Zias--one of the key forces behind Intuit's ground-breaking innovation program, has found a playful, artistic, and inspiring way to convey the principles of innovation that he has studied and discovered over years of personal application. Any individual or business can quickly absorb and retain a best practice in innovation by simply picking up this book and reading through the wealth of case studies, memorable analogies, and descriptive counsel. I highly recommend this book to any aspiring innovator!"

— **Curtis Lefrandt, CEO, Co-founder, Innovator's DNA**

What to Expect

From the "APE" to the "ZEBRA," The Innovation Animals is simply not your typical "principles for business success" book.

First, it has watercolors. And it has haiku.

Most important, this book invites you to take everything you think you know about business and dump it on the table. Mix it up. Turn it inside out.

The Innovation Animals explores real-life, real-world innovation situations—the wild successes and the cringe-worthy disasters—using clever acronyms such as …

— APE: Autonomy, Purpose, and Excellence
— IBIS: Inquiry-based Insightful Surprise
— PIG: Perseverance Ignites Growth

Each acronym encapsulates a lesson on how to think like an innovator, not like an accountant. In The Innovation Animals, you'll discover:

— How an insanely expensive manufacturing choice led to the revolutionary invention of the 2000s.
— The completely random circumstances that led to the development of masking tape.
— What happens when bad customer service gets set to music.
— Why big bosses may need to stay OUT of big decisions!
— And much more.

The Innovation Animals is colorful, pragmatic and just may change your life. And you'll finally know what a NENE is.

Foreword

Jeff and I have been colleagues and co-conspirators of innovation for almost a decade at Intuit, so it's a great honor to write this forward.

When I first met Jeff, he was leading a grassroots effort to pull together a group of employees for one of our first "hackathons." These hackathons, which we eventually started calling "Idea Jams," were so well received they provided the spark that lit a fire among Intuit's 8,000 employees.

Over the past decade and thanks in great part to Jeff's leadership, grassroots innovation has become a part of Intuit's innovation culture, including our flagship Unstructured Time program, which gives employees opportunity and freedom to pursue ideas that ignite their passion.

Through knowing Jeff, I've learned some important secrets of grassroots innovation that so many other people miss. First, leveraging grassroots innovation is the *best* way to engage employees so powerfully that work becomes more than work—it becomes a calling, an opportunity to make a difference.

Second—and even more important—in our experience, almost every great achievement and big new business started with grassroots innovation: A few employees had an idea, believed in it, and had the passion to make it happen. Our big successes such as SnapTax and GoPayment would not have happened without these passionate innovators.

Supporting our innovators' passion is Jeff's passion in life. In this book, you will experience his passion—albeit in a whimsical way—as he shares his wisdom and lessons learned about innovation best practices. I hope this book will stir your passion to innovate and make a difference.

— Hugh Molotsi,
Vice President, Intuit Labs Incubator
Mountain View, California

The Innovation Animals:
Innovation Lessons from A to Z

APE	Autonomy, Purpose, and Excellence
BULL	Business Under-utilizing Lateral Leadership
CAT	Commonly-avoided Terrain
DOG	Design Offers Growth
ELK	Excellent Leader's Kryptonite
FROGS	Frequent Re-examination of Objectives Guarantees Success
GIRAFFE	Greatness Involving Radical Autonomy Featuring Friendly Empathy
HIPPO	Highest-paid Person's Opinion
IBIS	Inquiry-based Insightful Surprise
JAGUAR	Jamming Almost Guarantees Upward-angled Results
KITE	Killer Insights Telegraph Excellence
LION	Life-giving Individualization Obstructs Naysayers
MOOSE	Market Orientation Obstructs Special Empathy
NENE	Nimble, Energized, Nervy Employees
OWL	Off-time's Well-known Liberation
PIG	Perseverance Ignites Growth
QUAIL	Quick, Unexpected Admonition Impairs Leadership
RAT	Radically Autonomous Team
SEAL	Seeking Empathy Amplifies Leadership
TIGER	Total Immersion Generates Excellent Results
URIAL	Under-represented Individual as Lead Customer
VIPER	Very Important Prioritized Experiments Rule
WHALE	Wise Hypotheses Actualize Lickety-split Experimentation
XEME	Xerox's Management Education
YAK	Year-over-year Appreciation and Kindness
ZEBRA	Zigzag Exploration Brings Resulting Awesomeness

Introduction

Steve Jobs was never one to hold back. Ever.

One of his primary passions was the truth and beauty that came from deep and broad-minded thinking. And Steve was about to impart some of this philosophy to a *Wired Magazine* reporter.

It was a foggy morning in 1996. The reporter drove down the San Francisco peninsula to meet with Steve at his NEXT Computer headquarters in Redwood City.

The interview could have quickly morphed into chest thumping about Pixar's giant hit *Toy Story* or the way the Macintosh had changed the world. But instead, Steve went in another direction. This leader of hi-tech's most secretive companies openly shared with *Wired* his best innovation *jujutsu*:

"Creativity is just connecting things. When you ask creative people how they did something, they feel a little guilty because they didn't really do it, they just saw something. It seemed obvious to them after a while. That's because they were able to connect experiences they've had and synthesize new things. And the reason they were able to do that was that they've had more experiences or they have thought more about their experiences than other people."[1]

Jobs had a passion for this concept, for making connections and for all of us, in our own best way, to help change the world.

This book, *The Innovation Animals*, asks you to immerse yourself and "work your mind," developing connections while having fun. Each chapter contains an animal watercolor, a *haiku* or *senryū*, and an innovation story. These three elements that comprise each chapter's innovation concepts are somewhat connected. But you, the reader, do the rest, connecting deeper concepts using your own perspective, your individual sense of priorities and, most importantly, your own strengths and passions.

- The painting at the beginning of each chapter should evoke a feeling. What is that feeling for you?
- The poem will either be a *haiku* or *senryū*, or a derivative of one of these styles.

The haiku style explores nature — often a season — and features a conceptual "jump cut" or juxtaposition in the middle so that you must make the connection between two different thoughts. *Senryū*, on the other hand, speak of the human condition and more boldly propose a human situation.

Going way out on a limb, these Japanese-style poems are a new form, "*HatsumeiKu*," or verse that is based on the haiku style but the stanzas explore how people invent. I don't expect that this new form will catch on with Japanese poetry purists, but I do want *haiku* aficionados to remain unoffended by my questionable poetic exploration.

The stories in each chapter describe an example of innovation, either one done poorly (a negative example) or done well (your innovation knights in shining armor).

Can you connect the feeling of the animal to the poem and to the story? More importantly, can you tap into your own passions and transform the connected elements into a durable meaning for *you*?

If so, you might find *The Innovation Animals* to be meaningful.

If it feels like an outline, kindling for the mind, or a breezy-yet-tangible simplification, then it just might be working.

Think of it this way:

- This book addresses human nature: How do we behave, and how do you behave? Choose your path and legacy.
- This book reveres nature: Will you love this world, life, and animals? I implore you to because, as far as I know, this is the only planet we all have.

APE

Autonomy, Purpose, and Excellence

Freedom will direct
a course so bold and vibrant,
the world stares in awe.

Andre was a scientist and loved his work, whether it was for pay or free. Of course, paid work took care of the bills, but he relished the sheer fun and emotional charge he got from doing unpaid work. Getting to explore the unknown. And his laboratory mates seemed to share his enthusiasm.

Little did Andre know that this fun, unpaid work was about to change his life forever.

Andre ran a research lab, and he and the postdoc fellows and research assistants had established a tradition called "Friday night experiments." The idea was simple: After all the regular work was done on Fridays, they tried out all the crazy, hair-brained, fun, wacky things they didn't get to do as part their regular jobs. As it turned out, roughly 10 percent of their research time was dedicated to these unplanned, unfunded investigations with no particular structure or expectation.

The researchers had started playing around with various materials, searching for breakthroughs at the atomic level. How could they compose structures that were thinner, stronger, and lighter than any other material seen before on Earth?

The applications of such technology would be numerous and powerful, but the boundaries of crystalline physical structures and other molecular-level binding seemed to have been entirely explored already. Sometimes, their research felt like driving 90 mph towards a dead end.

But frustration didn't set in; the promise of fun, snacks, little time pressure, and full autonomy beckoned each scientist to continue.

One Friday night, they decided to analyze a stack of carbon atoms by using adhesive tape to pull small clumps of graphite off a pencil lead. What they found was nothing short of astonishing: The extracted layer of graphite was incredibly thin. Andre and his research partner Konstantin proceeded to use tape to pull off layer after layer, and after repeating this exercise, what they had assembled was graphene: a single-atom-thick sheet of carbon that is light, strong, almost transparent, and an excellent conductor of electricity.[1]

This "impossible" task had been accomplished with nothing but pencil lead and short lengths of adhesive tape. These scientists had used $3 worth of materials and tools no more sophisticated than the average second grader would employ, yet graphene is 100 times stronger than steel—a single sheet can support an elephant—and has better conductivity than copper.

As you can imagine, great excitement followed the graphene discovery, and Andre Geim and Konstantin Novoselov published their study in 2004.

Fast forward to 2010. It was early morning, and Andre was getting prepared to leave for work. Rushing to quickly scarf some breakfast, grab some coffee, and iron a shirt, the phone rang. Andre picked up to hear a calm voice from Sweden: "Doctor Geim? You have won the Nobel Prize for physics!" The non-paid work had indeed paid off.

Connecting Concepts

In his seminal work on motivation titled *Drive*, Daniel Pink explores a framework of optimal human motivation in the context of creative work. Pink said that the main drivers of motivation are autonomy, purpose, and mastery. The invention of graphene, an outcome of the Geim-Novoselov Friday-night experiments, are a perfect example of amazing results growing out of a highly creative environment.

The Ape represents this archetype of creative motivation: Autonomy, Purpose, and Excellence. The freewheeling experiments at the Geim-Novoselov laboratory allowed the scientists and their students to be self-directed and experience the freedom of autonomy. Their shared sense of purpose—revolving around the powerful helix of discoveries that can make this a better world to live in—served as fuel for their continual curiosity. And they pursued excellence with a vengeance. Their dogged pursuit of better and better experiments, results, and beautiful, previously unimagined crystalline structures speaks for itself.

The Ape is a powerful, wild accelerant of our animal kingdom's creative force. Embrace the Ape.

BULL

Businesses Under-utilizing Lateral Leadership

*Stomping and spinning;
horns whipping with abandon,
foolish waste abounds.*

When Dave Carroll took his complaints with United Airlines to YouTube in the form of a fun and catchy trio of songs, he hoped to have one million hits … within a year.

What he got instead was an overnight sensation that proved one very important point to corporations worldwide: Social media has changed the game when it comes to customer service.

Before Facebook, Twitter, YouTube, and other social media channels became household words, there was an adage in business: When customers have a positive experience, they tell three friends. When they have a negative experience, they tell fourteen.

But in 2009, Dave Carroll told *100 million people* in every corner of the world—a PR disaster for the international carrier.

At the end of it all, the airline agreed to pay for the damages Dave had claimed, but the serious damage to their reputation was far more costly. And it could have been so easily avoided.

In 2008, Dave was a volunteer firefighter by day and struggling musician by night, touring areas around his hometown of Halifax, Nova Scotia, and beyond. He and his bandmates were headed to a gig in Omaha with a layover at Chicago's O'Hare Airport. While his plane was sitting on the tarmac in Chicago, Dave overheard a passenger behind him tell her companion that they were "throwing guitars out there!" The musicians quickly realized *their* guitars were being thrown and alerted United employees, but they were met with indifference at every turn.[1] When he realized the next day that his Taylor guitar—valued at $3,500—had been seriously damaged by the airline's handlers, he attempted to file a complaint.

Dave spent the next nine months speaking with and emailing an assortment of United customer service agents, all to no avail. Everyone he talked to was completely ambivalent about his situation, claiming they were "unable" to assist him because his claim didn't meet the airline's policy standards.

This poor customer service was the result of employees not being allowed to take ownership of the situation. Each one passed him off to another and another until finally, he was informed that his claim was being denied due to "company policy." He would receive no further responses from the airline.

So, what did he do? He wrote a song about it and uploaded it to YouTube.

The video went viral, clocking 150,000 hits in just one day and half a million hits within three days, sparking intense media attention. United's stock started to tank, and while some say it was just a fluke, it's hard to imagine that a viral video called "United Breaks Guitars" had absolutely nothing to do with it.[2]

The airline did finally offer compensation to Dave and claimed they'd learned their lesson, even requesting permission to use the video as a training tool. However, for Dave Carroll, it wasn't about money. He even asked United to donate the money to charity. He really wanted the airline to own up about how it had damaged his property and then given him the run-around.

All of the bad publicity could have been avoided if just one employee had been empowered—given the authority to make a decision that showed Dave he was a respected and valued customer. However, they were run over by the Bull: <u>B</u>usinesses <u>U</u>nder-utilizing <u>L</u>ateral <u>L</u>eadership.

Connecting Concepts

The Bull, a business that under-utilizes the potentially astonishing power of its employees, truly does destroy china shops (as well as most other high-value environments). When you see the Bull, you know that the company has squandered the power of permitting employees to be creative, enticing employees to improve customer's lives, and encouraging employees to routinely make speedy, effective decisions at the lowest possible level.

The "Bull organization" is slow, headstrong, entirely lacking empathy, and begs you to grab a big shovel to clean up the inevitable messes the bull leaves behind.

Like the rodeo rider who clings to the saddle until the Bull has expended its last surge of destructive, misguided energy, you—the courageous and effective innovator—must defeat the Bull.

CAT

Commonly-avoided Terrain

Skewing status quo,
pushing previous visions
beyond former fears.

The two friends were dreamers, and they dreamed big. Their approach was unusual, but avoiding the well-worn path was typical for them. As two hard-working graduate students, they often questioned the very paradigms they were being taught.

These two young men were Sergey Brin and Larry Page, co-founders of Google. They had the crazy idea of creating a better search engine. Ridiculous! Search engines already existed; top minds from competing companies had already tuned and evolved algorithms beyond normal human achievement. Not to mention, there seemed to be no revenue possibilities from such a pursuit. Category leader AltaVista had yet to make a single dollar from its search engine, even as mega amperes of current flowed through their bays of supercomputers.

Paul Graham, founder of Y-Combinator, has characterized this phenomenon in his brilliant blog: "The best ideas seem nearly impossible, or crazy, or both ..."

The primary motivator of terrain "avoidance" is fear, which comes in a few shades:[3]

- The path seems too difficult.
- Predecessors have tried and failed.
- The path is just plain CRAZY.

Connecting Concepts

The Cat—Commonly-avoided Terrain—is a script in need of a flip. In other words, if an innovator is smart enough, passionate enough, and filled with enough insight to attack a commonly-avoided area of invention, they have actually created a significant advantage for themselves. Some of these avoided areas constitute the largest, ripest and—ultimately—best business opportunities to be found.

Cats inspire extremes. To a "cat person," they are fuzzy companions, noble and elegant, a gift from God; to cat haters, they are cold, self-serving, allergy-provoking, and shred furniture.

Such is commonly-avoided terrain. Some places can kill you, they're so dangerous, yet to really break through, you must go there ... whether it is the improbable-looking climb or the terrain that enables crazy, entirely implausible exploration.

Mass assumptions across entire industries can be simply, purely wrong:

"You can't make money by giving stuff away for free."

"Nobody can make money on music content anymore; it is all pirated."

"The tablet will never sell; it's big and clunky, the worst of a laptop and a mobile phones."

Conventional wisdom can hinder the innovator.

We embrace the Cat. Go where others have turned chicken! Find the open spots where the pragmatic (yet weak) have turned and run. The rough, scary, interesting terrain that screams "GO AWAY!" to others now beckons you, the bold and creative innovator, who can claim, reap, sow, and harvest from these rocky ridges.

Innovation

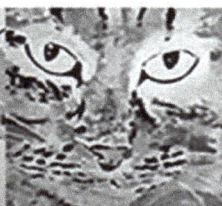

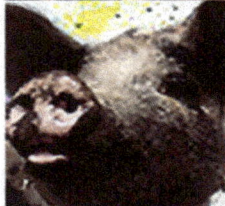

Animals

DOG

Designing Offers Growth

Experiments start;

Broad ideas, narrow focus,

Deep, deep empathy.

When Intuit founder Scott Cook tells the story of how successful agri-tech platform Fasal came to be, he is quick to point out that if it had been up to the bosses at his company, the platform would have never seen the light of day.

Although the company was looking for a way to improve the financial status of the Indian people, when one of their teams suggested an idea to work with farmers — nearly half the country's population — they were given a solid thumbs-down. However, Intuit's culture of allowing employees the opportunity to prove their ideas through experimentation soon paid off. Fasal's surprisingly simple concept caught on with India's farmers and has helped more than one million of them within the past four years.

Now here's the backstory ...

While company executives were exploring India's rural areas for ways to improve the economic lives of everyday workers, they stumbled upon a longstanding and growing problem:

Caught in a rainstorm at a bus shelter, they struck up a conversation with some local residents. The farmers told them that they often failed to make a profit on their crops, and sometimes actually lost money, for lack of a simple, efficient and timely way to target the best market for their goods.

Once a crop was harvested and ready for sale, the farmer could make only a best guess as to which local market would be paying the best price for his goods. Sometimes, he would get information from other growers, but that word-of-mouth advice was often outdated or otherwise unreliable.

So, usually he would take his goods first to, for example, a market a few miles to the north. Meanwhile, at a market just a few miles farther away to the south, he might have found a wholesaler who was willing to pay 20% more for that same crop. Although the price differential could be chalked up to simple demand — the buyer in the north had ample supply whereas the one in the south had none – why couldn't the farmer just refuse the northern buyer's low bid and go with the southern wholesaler?

Due to the perishable nature of fresh crops, it was a very risky bet to assume that another market would pay more. He might even get to the southern market only to find out they were paying even less for his produce, which would now be another day or two old. He would also have to absorb the cost of getting his crop from one market to another. All of this added to up to unstable prices for farmers as well as unstable supplies for buyers. What the farmers needed was a reliable way to keep up with current market prices.

The Intuit team began to brainstorm ways they could help fix the situation. Their notion of design thinking was important to this problem-solving process: deep empathy, going from broad to go narrow, and rapid experimentation with customers would be critical factors in finding a way to help the farmers.

Many of the growers didn't have Internet access, so web-based data was not the solution. Nearly all of the farmers had cell phones, however, and nearly all of those phones were able to send and receive SMS messages.

The designers performed a quick and inexpensive experiment to test out an idea. Over a few weeks, they recruited a test group of farmers to whom they would send manual texts on a daily basis, detailing what each market needed and how much the local *mandis* — the market middlemen — were willing to pay. Intuit employees went from market to market, mandi to mandi, asking questions and passing the knowledge they gained on to their group of "early-adopter" farmers.

It quickly became evident that they were on to something big. The 110 pilot participants reported a 16% increase in the prices they were able to get for their hard work. The mandis were also happy because they wound up with a much more predictable source of fresher, higher-quality goods.

Over the next few months, the team built a full-scale product using complex algorithms that can acquire and disseminate information several times a day to provide the most personalized and up-to-date data to the farmer via automated text.

Fasal, which means "harvest" in Hindi, grew quickly through word-of-mouth and now has more than a million subscribers. It has been monetized through advertising, thereby keeping it free to users and all the more valuable to its user base.

By using broad thinking and a quick, inexpensive set of experiments in their design process, Intuit was able to empower a large group of people in a very short timeframe. By providing employees the opportunity to pursue ideas that the higher-ups had initially doubted, the company has now improved the lives of countless Indian families. This kind of leadership promotes ingenuity and brings out the creative thinker in all employees, which often translates into improving people's lives.

Connecting Concepts

The Dog (Design Offers Growth) teaches us that proper thinking about design – the type of design that connects with the heart, leverages rapid experimentation, and invokes broad, powerful thinking – can change people's lives forever.

ELK

Excellent Leader's Kryptonite

The leader succumbs
to bleak, destructive darkness,
and teams fail to thrive.

Xeena walked into the room, and the team thought, *This will be nothing but trouble.*

"Hey everybody!" Xeena shouted, "We need the monthly TBCW reports to be done early this time, I mean for the whole department, within the next hour. Let's go."

The team was upset, but not surprised, by her proclamation and directive. Would she follow now with the typical threats, even as idle as they may usually be?

"Come on, children … ha, ha! I mean, people! Let's go! This is the most important thing now."

Harlan thought, *Well this sucks. Even if I get it done on time, then she'll take the credit.*

Harlan and the team got started on the reports, but half an hour later, Xeena came back and said, "OK, everybody, we need this done in the new format. Yeah. I had this great idea to improve the report format. Use this Word template … wait a minute … where did I put that?"

Fighting every fiber in his body, heart, and mind, Harlan decided to push back a bit. "Wait a minute. We need more advance warning … that doesn't make any sense … can we just talk this over for a little bit?"

Xeena scoffed, "Come on now! Just get with it, you know? I know you don't like change … this is just a change. It's going out, Harlan."

Of course, the scenario above is nothing more than a ridiculous, over-the-top illustration of poor management behavior. But, recent research from Harvard professor and director of research Teresa Amabile and psychology researcher Steven Kramer [Amabile 2011] has shown that, in this scenario, our fictitious manager Xeena has actually nailed the four most atrocious characteristics of bad leaders. The research shows that people really are experiencing this type of leadership incompetence out there in the wild.[1]

Professors Amabile and Kramer researched this topic for 15 years. Investigating what makes people happy and productive at work, they collected diaries from more than 280 professionals in seven different companies. They studied the results of these daily digital diaries and found the results surprising.

The researchers found that during one-third of the 12,000 days of data collected, people indicated they were entirely unhappy and demotivated at work. The research then led them to a study of root causes, which identified the culprits. You guessed it! The key to this problem was bad bosses.

It was clear that bosses should be raising employee's confidence, giving them freedom and pushing them to prosper. But, for the most part, this was not happening.

So, if you've wondered what the true Kryptonite to great leadership is, you need look no further. The study shows that the most solid mechanisms for robbing employees of all motivation, esteem, and capability of producing results for customers boils down to these four potent "doses" of Kryptonite:

- Squelch all pride of accomplishment.
- Block employees' progress.
- Credit yourself for all the work.
- Ignore signals and messages from the team.

No Pride of Accomplishment

One of most frustrating yet inevitable aspects of many people's jobs is setbacks. The only thing that can really overcome the irritation of setbacks is the celebration of small wins as milestones and sub-milestones are achieved. Conversely, the way to block out all pride of accomplishment is for a leader to harp on setbacks and steal moments of pride around wins.[2]

Block Employees' Progress

Whereas the absolute best leaders will block interference for their employees, give them cover, and actively remove obstacles, a poor leader will constantly be in the way. Since one of the primary motivators for employees is achievement and mastery, by blocking progress, the leader can really strike at the heart of an employee's motivational system.

Credit Yourself for the Work

To really make an employee's life feel meaningless, make sure all the credit goes to you as the leader. Credit-hogging—and the anger and pain it engenders—is more of the most efficient ways to alienate everyone around you.

Ignore Messages from the Team

The power of wishful thinking is a kissing-cousin to denial. The best way to remain out of touch with your team—and avoid any meaningful leadership whatsoever—is to constantly deny and bury messages from the team regarding areas of improvement. As Amabile mocks in the research study, "There is no morale problem in *this* company. And for anybody who thinks there is, we have a nice, big bus waiting outside to take you wherever you want to look for work."

Connecting Concepts

Now you've seen the key elements of bad leadership. This leadership kryptonite kills motivation, engagement, and progress. Our Elk, in this context, should be avoided.

So what are the drivers of excellent leadership? Well, how about the opposite of the kryptonite? Trust, drive, encouraging vision, empathy, humility, and mentorship are some of these "opposites" that exemplify good leadership and may take a boss' leadership to the next level.

FROGS

Frequent Re-examination of Objectives
Guarantees Success

Capture my eye you?
distraction! turn and leave now.
priorities win.

Mark Twain famously said, "If the first thing you do each morning is to eat a live frog, you can go through the day with the satisfaction of knowing that that is probably the worst thing that is going to happen to you all day long." [1]

Do what's most important and forget the rest.

Your priorities could be thought of as everything from big, ugly frogs to small frogs and mere tadpoles. Most of us tend to dive in and eat the small frogs and tadpoles because, hey, they're easy to get out of the way.

But that is exactly what you *don't* want to do if ultimate effectiveness and success is your goal.

Eat That Frog, a great book on time management by Brian Tracy, asserts that a detailed breakdown of priorities is essential in achieving success.

All of us have many more things to do than we will ever get done. This is just a fact—get over it! What we should do is think about the Pareto Principle: the 80/20 rule, also known as the law of the vital few, and how it applies to your to-do list.

Even under light scrutiny, we can see that only about 20 percent of the things we do are truly important. In fact, the most important 20 percent may actually be 10 to 100 times more important to us than the remaining 80 percent on the list!

Prioritize your to-do list. Focus on the big frogs first. You'll find that all the tiny frogs and tadpoles—the 80 percent—may not be worth doing at all.

Eat the big, ugly frogs first thing every day. This helps you stay focused on the most important things, those things that can make or break your personal and professional success. When you re-evaluate what's most important, you can develop the best plan for overall effectiveness.

Time Away from Firefighting

But how do you even know what's most important? How can you achieve excellent frog identification?

Edward Hess, author of *Smart Growth*, interviewed numerous successful small-business and startup entrepreneurs who found clever ways to grow their businesses. He discovered that they were able to think strategically about what their priorities should be.

Two themes emerged: One, most daily activities felt like fighting fires, and two, moments of clarity and insight came only when they took a clean break from "firefighting."

We all need to take some time to get away from fires and see where the biggest frogs are. Reserve an afternoon each week to think about your business' chief priorities. [2]

Make the Journey

The other key to eating those big frogs is to both subdivide the big frog and persevere over time. You've heard the adage that the way to eat an elephant (or the biggest, ugliest frogs in our case) is one small bite at a time. The metaphor disgusts me … but the lesson is spot-on.

I recall one business trip to Manhattan where my meetings for the day were mainly in Soho (at the southernmost point of the island). However, due to other plans during that trip, my hotel was on the Upper East Side—90 blocks away. I asked a Manhattan-based coworker if I should take the subway or cab or—since I had been eating way too much on the trip (not to mention sitting on my rear end in meetings the whole time)— if I could walk the distance. He said, "No problem; you can walk it. Those are short blocks."

I liked the sound of that! Short blocks. What if I just took one block at a time, did a mini-celebration (in my mind, that is; no public dancing) after each block? Eat that 90-block frog one block at a time?

As you might have guessed, I survived the walk with nary a side ache nor pulled hamstring. It was a fun and refreshing city hike, not to mention that I felt a bit proud of myself.

Connecting Concepts

So, keep these three tips in mind to know what your priorities are and how to execute them:

- Reserve time to correctly identify your biggest frogs (top priorities).
- Eat the biggest, ugliest frog first thing each morning.
- If the frog is enormous, eat it one small bite at a time.

GIRAFFE

Greatness Involving Radical Autonomy Featuring Friendly Empathy

The depth of delight
holds savannah's torrid impact
as hearts warm and meld.

"Joshie the Giraffe" is best friend to Chris Hurn's young son. So, when Chris' family came back from their holiday at the Ritz-Carlton on Amelia Island in Florida only to find out that Joshie had been left behind, you can imagine their distress. Chris improvised, telling his son that Joshie was having a little extra holiday, and he phoned the Ritz-Carlton to report the mishap.

That same evening, the Ritz-Carlton called to inform them that Joshie had been found in the laundry and had been handed over to the hotel's Loss Prevention Team. Chris also told them about the story he concocted to appease his son and requested that they take a picture of Joshie on a chair by the pool to serve as proof. Much to his relief and delight, the staff agreed.

But that just the beginning of the story.

The package containing Joshie arrived a couple of days later. But there was more to it than just Joshie's safe return—the Ritz-Carlton staff had kept going. Inside the package were some Ritz-Carlton-branded goodies including a Frisbee and a football.

More importantly, there was also a binder that meticulously documented Joshie's extended stay at the hotel. The binder contained pictures of Joshie sunbathing by the pool, having a relaxing massage, and meeting other "cuddly friends." One picture showed Joshie driving to the beach in a buggy! They even snapped a picture of Joshie working on the security cameras, making sure that other important belongings and "best friends" didn't get lost or left behind.

Clearly, the Ritz-Carlton staff not only met the Chris' expectations, they exceeded them by a wide margin! As it turns out, all Ritz-Carlton personnel are given a $2000 budget to be used *as they see fit* to serve visitors' customer service needs. Because the staff is given such *autonomy* by the management, even entry-level customer service agents can act instantly and creatively to meet customers' needs.

Lengthy approval processes have been replaced with trust, self-direction, autonomy, purpose, and empathy in action.

So how do you know if a service exceeds customer expectations? Joshie and the Ritz teach us the six ingredients of customer delight:

1. Get the customer to say "*wow.*"
2. Be spontaneous and unexpected.
3. Personalize each message and interaction.
4. Make sure the customer feels valued.
5. Leverage authentic and pure empathy.
6. Build and tell a compelling story.

Amazing customer service is a critical and valued asset in any business. When the customers are satisfied, not only will they go back to use the service again, they will flip over to become enthusiastic promoters of the service or good. This is free—and powerful—advertising for your company. [1]

Connecting Concepts

Customer service, delight, and creative solutions to problems are all about exceeding the customers' expectations. And talk about exceeding expectations! There is nothing like the Ritz-Carlton Hotel story to demonstrate radical autonomy where management asks each employee to think, lead, and delight every day.

The giraffe shows us that radical autonomy coupled with authentic empathy can produce astonishing results. Not to mention, can you put a price tag on serving up an experience that a child will remember for the rest of his life? This story teaches us that there is nothing better a business can do for its customers and society at large than to wow customers by serving with joy while exceeding their expectations.

Innovation

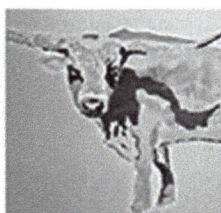

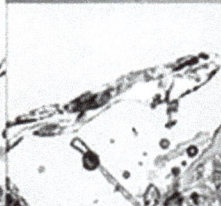

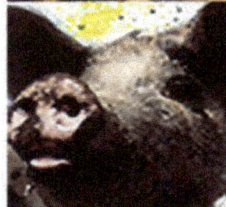

Animals

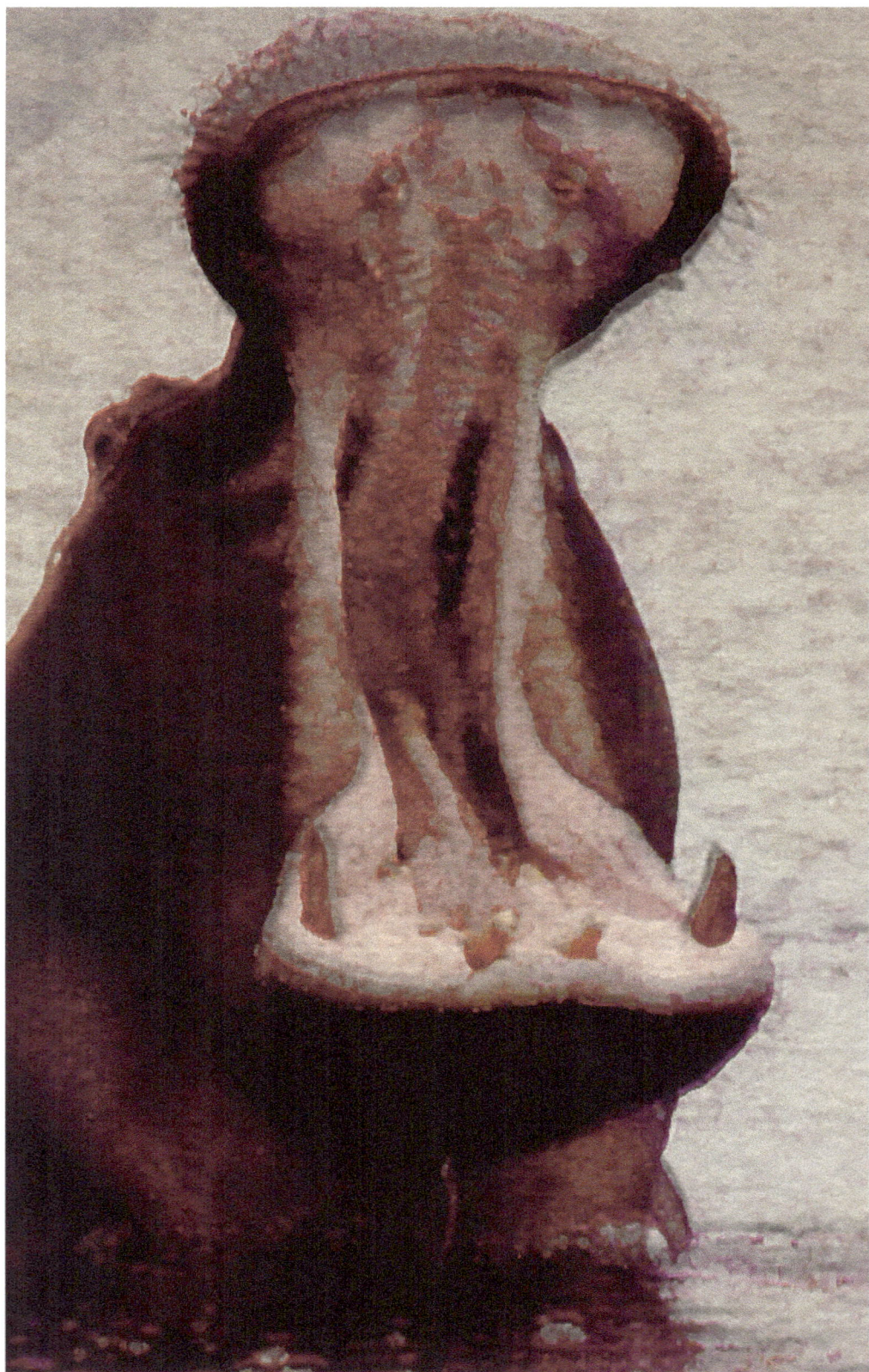

HiPPO

Highest-paid Person's Opinion

Opinions, not fact
line the express lane, passion
morphing to regret.

The "HiPPO," perhaps the best known of all animal acronyms in business, is truly the inspiration for this book. "HiPPO" stands for "Highest-paid Person's Opinion."

We've all seen it: Leaders who are always ready to weigh in with their deep knowledge and hair-trigger decision-making—not to mention a huge cache of opinions on any and every subject.

Many have pointed out the serious implications of that HiPPO dropping in, whether early or late in projects, to spew forth opinions. When the HiPPO is so much higher than you on the workplace totem pole, the pressure and "physics" of the HiPPO's weight creates an exceedingly powerful force.

The HiPPO rumbles by every now and again to give opinions about what you should be doing—that you're not—to drive project success. You feel like you *must* consider the idea even if it's crazy, disruptive, difficult to achieve, or way late to the party.

So, you must figure something out! But how can you deal with that HiPPO?

Let's imagine the following scenario. (Although if this looks like your workplace on a monthly, weekly or—heaven forfend—*daily* basis, imagination will *not* be required.)

A number of years ago, I was leading development of a new feature for a popular software product. We had to choose from among several strategies for piloting the feature with target customers. We started small, tested with users, and were continuing with our testing, agile iteration, and feature rollout plans. Then it came time to meet with upper management for a program review.

The HiPPO decision handed down in that review ignored *all* of our suggestions and data. The leader instructed us to go for the grand slam: releasing the feature, as is, to the million-plus customer base within a quarter.

You just need to wander down your hall, or any workplace hall, and hear similar stories.

So, are you wondering what happened? Well, the feature really wasn't quite right for customers yet—as the team already knew—so when it rolled out to millions with the HiPPO's high expectations for increased up-sales, the feature fell flat on its face. Six months later, it was canceled because the project, of course, had missed all HiPPO-mandated revenue targets.

But, to reiterate, the boss thought the feature was ready and would naturally be an outstanding success. Ultimately, what could have evolved into a $30 million yearly premier up-sell had quickly become a goose egg.

So, when that HiPPO comes around stirring up the dust (figuratively or literally), if you haven't mastered effective pushback or "HiPPO taming" skills, you are in big trouble.

How can you deal? Anathema to HiPPOs is *lean experimentation.*

Lean experimentation will automatically classify any opinion as a useful assumption that should be tested on customers. By evangelizing and modeling the language of lean experimentation, you are creating a meritocracy of "learning via measurement of customer behavior." Stand tall and be proud because your approach will not only help yourself with HiPPOs, it can teach everyone around you, even HiPPOs, a better way of working!

Connecting Concepts

Given all this, here is your HiPPO-tamer playbook:
- When the HiPPO approaches, don't run. They will just give an earth-rumbling chase.
- Smile! The HiPPO likes friendlies who (also) love their ideas.
- When the HiPPO boldly weighs in with their 100-percent opinion (0-percent fact), continue to smile and say, "That's a great idea! Thank you."
- And then, very quickly, without taking another breath, say "Let's test that. We will test that with customers!"

Note: in the software product example above, in retrospect, we could have proposed to test at a small scale but within the big channel that our HiPPO was excited about. If we had committed to increasing the customer reach incrementally, based on a set of experiments, we could have avoided accepting the exact HiPPO directive.

So, remember:
- Keep smiling.
- Keep learning by observing customer behavior.
- Keep making true progress.

You now have learned how to tame HiPPOs. In fact, you are transforming HiPPOs into Apes without them even knowing it. (You've retained autonomy, are driving for excellence, and are true to your purpose, correct?)

And as an owner of HiPPO taming skills, you and your fellow HiPPO-masters -- one fine day -- shall be the key, masterful rangers of successful innovation environments.

IBIS

Invention by Insight and Surprise

Insights pull you up,
soaring higher than ever,
broad vision so clear.

Throughout his career, Alexander Fleming proved himself to be a dedicated researcher who searched tirelessly for answers to medical questions. He'd won a scholarship to study in London at St. Mary's Hospital Medical School, and after earning his degree in bacteriology, he was awarded a staff position under the head of the Inoculation Department.

As a result of his zeal for scientific inquiry, he became known by his peers as a keen researcher. However, even his strongest supporters remarked that he kept a horrendously messy lab. Petri dishes containing bacteria samples would always pile up as their keeper pursued his goal of finding ways to improve medical science.

In 1928, Fleming was studying staphylococcus, a form of bacteria that was routinely wreaking havoc in those days. It caused everything from painful boils on the skin to debilitating and often fatal infections, particularly in those with weakened immune systems. Fleming's experiments required him to cultivate samples of the bacteria and its properties with the ultimate goal of finding a way to eradicate it.

By late summer, temperatures in London were rising and the doctor decided that a couple of weeks out of the city were in order. He hastily piled the Petri dishes filled with staph cultures onto a bench in the corner of his lab and left for a family vacation.

What he found when he got back would dramatically change the way infections were treated in the world.

Fleming noticed, upon arrival back at the lab, that while a good portion of the bacteria appeared unchanged, an area in each dish was filled with mold. Mold! How could this be?

Fleming took the surprise seriously. Upon deeper investigation, he discovered that in the area surrounding the mold, the staph had been either destroyed or prevented from developing.

He quickly realized he'd benefitted from an amazing happenstance. A nearby lab was investigating different molds, and a mold spore, carried through the air, managed to find its way into Fleming's bacteria samples. The unmonitored temperature conditions in his lab also had proved serendipitous. If the cultures had been placed in an incubator, it is likely that only the bacteria would have survived. As it was, the environment was suitable for both the mold and the bacteria to endure until Fleming's return.

After isolating and identifying the growth as a Penicillium mold, Fleming began to work on ways to produce the "mold juice," as he called it, in pure form and in larger quantities so that it could be used to treat common illnesses such as pneumonia and meningitis. Although he struggled with extracting the substance that he finally named "penicillin," it was through his experiments and observations that researchers were later able to develop ways to cultivate and administer it in mass quantities.

Although history describes Alexander Fleming's discovery of penicillin as "accidental," knowing the whole story shows how his dedication to scientific inquiry, deep and detailed observation, and experimentation gave us one of the most important medical advancements in human history.

Connecting Concepts

One of the most important lessons in all of science is "savor the surprises." Fleming, a bit sloppy in his housekeeping, was a great observer of all things experimental. We thus find that the Ibis is a bird that supports and prioritizes the essence of this keen observation, an embrace of surprises, and appreciation of deep inquiry.

Innovation

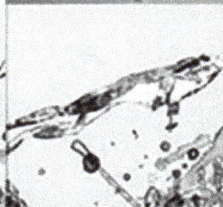

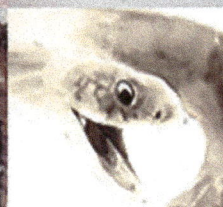

Animals

JAGUAR

Jamming Almost Guarantees Ultimately Awesome Results

Time, place and focus,
now so clear, as jamming is
work, play, truth and life.

When Intuit executives decided to roll out their new "whitespace" program, they didn't realize what they were about to get into.

The whitespace idea was sparked by a best practice from neighboring company Google. Google was already famous for its program that allows Google employees to spend 20 percent of their time working on projects of their own choosing. This type of corporate "self-directed work time" program was not even a Google invention: Companies such as 3M and Hewlett-Packard had utilized similar programs for years.

Intuit wanted to try it out and began offering employees a slightly more conservative 10-percent program. The term "whitespace" was used as a metaphor to indicate free, unbooked segments of time. The program first rolled out across Inuit's Small Business Division, where QuickBooks was the major product offering. It would start with the engineering group and then branch out from there.

The plan was simple: Engineering leaders would send notes to the whole division, encouraging employees to use this new program. They would be able to do something other than their usual assignments during their 10-percent time—they could innovate, do new things in new ways.

The notes went out, and the new whitespace program seemed to be a good thing, a wonderful idea on paper, yet it suffered from a key problem: No one was using it.

As an engineering manager in the Small Business Payroll Group, I volunteered to drive the whitespace program for our section. We'd noticed that people weren't latching onto this whitespace idea, so I went around and talked to employees to see what the problem might be.

It wasn't hard to quickly pick up a number of clues. Questions such as "How do I do it?", "How am I going to find the right thing to work on?" and "I'm really busy now, so how could I possibly find time?" were popping up. People were confused.

But we soon stumbled upon a breakthrough. A young engineer on my team, Zach, had just come back from spending the weekend at a Yahoo! event called "Hack Day." Zach was fired up about the experience:

"It was awesome," he said. "We worked all night long doing whatever we wanted, and we were slinging some serious code. Then the next day, we went around the room. People stood up and in 90 seconds shouted out what they had done, holding up their laptop and showing a quick demo. It was amazing."

Zach and the rest of our team discussed the merits of Yahoo! Hack Day and talked about doing our own version. It seemed like a great idea. But the deeper we got into planning, the clearer it became that doing an overnight Hack Day on the weekend, for programmers only, may not be the best thing for Intuit.

Even so, some of the Yahoo! lessons were clear: Holding a fun event where people compete could be engaging and energizing. Putting together something tangible with rules and a specific time on the calendar seemed powerful. What other way could better address the issue of this whitespace thing being "nebulous and open-ended"? A Hack Day, or something like it, would give some *bones* to the program: Employees would be clear on how to approach their whitespace with a specific time, place, and goal.

So, we decided to put together our own Hack Day for the QuickBooks payroll engineering employees. We worked with leadership, got buy-in from our general manager down, and dove into planning the event. We decided on a three-day contest, in the middle of the week, and set things up so people could really go deep with their ideas.

As the date got closer, our VP of development suggested a two-day event. Then a week before the event, the same VP came back to me and said, "Hey, can we make this jam [which we were calling "Hacktivism" at the time] just one day long—there's a lot of pressure about taking this much time away from regular work."

I thought it over and, realizing this was essentially an experiment, said that we'd figure out how to make a one-day format work.

A few days before the Hacktivism event, *again*, this same leader said to me, "Hey ... can we just call this off? It's a big investment of time to take the whole division and spend a day doing this."

I decided this was one of these situations where feigning insensitivity could be "useful." I said, "I think it will be fine; we'll just go ahead and do it." This VP of product development—my boss' boss—looked at me a little funny. But the approach seem to work as he didn't push back, and I can only imagine he made a decision at that moment to just let the cards fall where they may.

The day of Hacktivism arrived. Sure enough, most of the division showed up, and we had enough of a set agenda to keep people moving and innovating. Although this turned out to be a weak first effort compared with later jams, the event was an overall success with people dipping their toes into the innovation waters. We were collaborating, brainstorming, pitching, and winning silly prizes, all in one day.

What we saw that day was that a tangible event—on the calendar—gave people a way to move innovations forward. Over time, we realized that these events were becoming a foundational aspect of our innovation culture.

We changed the name from Hacktivism to "Idea Jams" to make the events friendlier and more mainstream for all attendees. We also helped teams devise different types of jams. Within a year or two, we had Pain Jams, Solution Jams, Code Jams, Patent Jams, Design Jams and—later on—even Launch Jams, Copy Writing Jams, and Design for Delight Jams.

As our "jamming expertise" increased, we learned how to purposefully connect the jams together (sort of) Lego-style. By configuring different sequences of jams for different teams, we found efficient and easy-to-describe ways of driving results, all the way from initial idea to new official offerings being used by customers. We discovered that employees benefit from tangible, specific innovation events and challenges, and we realized their dream of changing the corporate culture. From a simple dream, we were able to leverage jams to the point that more than one employee has been overheard saying, "Well, to get that done, let's jam."

Connecting Concepts

Jams provide an easy-to-spot on-ramp to Unstructured Time (what we previously called whitespace). Not only that, jams can be designed to add just enough structure—without diminishing autonomy, mastery and purpose—to help innovative teams move all the way from a back-of-the-napkin idea to shipping customer-delighting products.

The Jaguar teaches us the merits of jamming, a cornerstone concept for a nimble, grassroots innovation system. The Jaguar leads us down the twisting, obscured jungle path towards the desired destination. Follow the Jaguar.

KITE

Kill-shot Introspection Transforms Execution

Time freezes moments
of vicious devastation,
insight emerging.

Jake Harriman was a Marine.

Tall, strong—and normally fearless—Jake embodied the leatherneck archetype. But here in his fighting hole in Iraq, Jake was 90 seconds away from the most terrifying and tragic moment of his life.

Jake Harriman grew up in West Virginia learning the value of sacrifice and hard work. After attending the U.S. Naval Academy, he joined the Marines and was trained as an infantry commander and joined the special forces of the U.S. Marines Recon Unit.

After graduation, Jake became a platoon commander in infantry and a special operations member. After the Sept. 11 attacks, he went to Africa on anti-terrorism missions, and in 2003, he went to the front lines of the Iraqi invasion.

On that fateful day in Iraq, Jake and his platoon were in their fighting holes, arrayed in a defensive position facing north. Jake jumped out of his hole to check his troop's lines.

He saw a white car coming up the road towards them. They all raised their guns; chances were the car was a suicide bomber. The car stopped far short of their position. A man jumped out and began running towards them. Perhaps the bombs were strapped to his body? Jake and his platoon braced themselves. Just then, a large black military truck came up behind the white car. U.S. troops jumped out of the truck and sprayed the car with bullets.

At that moment, Jake realized what was happening. Iraqi Special Forces had been coercing poor farmers to use guns and bombs to fight the Americans ... or else their wives and children would be raped and killed in front of them.

He sprinted towards the white car, realizing that this poor farmer had been coming to the Americans for *help*. The farmer turned to run back to his car, screaming and waving his arms.

When Jake reached the white car, the man was holding the blood-soaked body of his daughter. His wife lay in the passenger seat, dead of a gunshot wound and holding their small baby, also dead from shots to the chest and head.

The look in the man's eyes was unforgettable.

Jake lowered his weapon to his side—something he'd never done before—and began to weep with the farmer. Jake looked up to the sky, hoping to God for some answer as to what he could do.

He realized that there are, and always will be, bad people in this world. These bad people will always be able to use and coerce the poor, the desperate, the powerless.

Jake, in his heart and mind, knew at that moment that the only way to end terrorism is to end extreme poverty.

He loves the Marines and he loves his country, but after being forced into the depths of root-cause analysis that few of us will ever experience, he realized his life would best be dedicated to ending extreme poverty. Out of this passion for social good, high-impact ideas, and effective execution of these ideas, he has set out to enable his vision via the Nuru International non-profit organization.

Connecting Concepts

The Kite stands for Kill-shot Introspection Transforms Execution. No one wants to experience this sort of tragedy or even highly dramatic circumstances, yet the utter severity of the Kite's impact can drive helpful change.

When the Kite appears, we have the opportunity to reevaluate our beliefs. In the case of Jake Harriman, his reevaluation triggered the following thoughts:

- What is my purpose in life?
- Will my planned actions help achieve my true, purpose-backed vision?

- What is the deepest root cause of the problem I am addressing?
- Do I still believe in my current mission? Does it attack true root causes?
- Is there a better way to make my optimal contribution?

Given the power of the Kite, if and when it appears, let us embrace its transformational energy. Like Jake, you may find that a reassessment helps you pivot to a new approach. The Kite is a double-edged sword, one that can hurt innovators as well as shake them up in a manner that transforms the world in which we live.

LION

Life-giving Individualization Obstructs Naysayers

One person's true key unlocks magical doors to joy, awe, and respect.

Fifteen-year-old Richie Parker's eyes grew wide as he gazed upon his dream, the absolute object of his desires: a 1964 Chevy Impala SS.

Let's face it: The 64' Impala SS, a big ol' classic American muscle car, would fire up any teenage boy who had established himself as a "car guy." Yet *this* story of desire—the historic Impala plus a yearning to drive the car—is an unusual one.

You see, Richie Parker has no arms.

Richie was born with a genetic condition called *bilateral amelia*. Simply put, he was born without arms. His father, Tracy, recalled being told his son's condition:

"I was just sort of dumbfounded, like, what do you mean?" However, the second he saw his son, everything changed. "He [was] the cutest baby. The cutest little boy. After about five minutes, all I could say was, 'When can I take my kid home?'"

Richie's mother, Lotti, was another driving force in Richie's development. She believed more than anything in having a positive, strong, and creative mindset.

When she got the news of Richie's birth defect, her mind immediately went into action. She didn't waste any time focusing on what her son was missing; she instead thought about how the family would manage the complexities of Richie's condition, things such as how to open doors or get dressed or eat a meal.

"When I saw Richie, I knew there [was] no question. We wanted his childhood to be as close to any other child's as possible," she said.

Richie was never held back from opportunities and activities. Said Richie's father, "The other kids in the neighborhood had bikes, and we were set on Richie riding a bike." So, they figured out a way for Richie to independently ride a bicycle, which turned out to be a very important stepping stone to Richie's enthusiasm for anything with wheels.

Being able to ride a bike by himself only enhanced Richie Parker's sense of independence. Later, as a teenager, he worked on and then drove cars. He fell in love with them, in fact, and knew that his life's work would have something to do with these wonderful machines.

So, back to the Chevy Impala.

When Richie saw the car, it was sheer love. He would do anything to be able to work on and drive such a fine automobile. So eight years ago, he decided to apply for a job Hendrick Motorsports.

Hendrick engineering manager Rex Stump thought it over and then invited Richie to join the team as an intern. Said Stump: "I [knew] he would get everything [done that] needed to [be] done, it was more question in my mind of how."

Richie's internship, originally set to last 10 months, transformed into a career. Eight years and five championships later, Richie is still there as an engineer designing chassis and body components and working across all four of the company's race teams.

Richie uses his feet to handle tools as well drive the cars. And he's one of the highest performers anyone has ever seen. Not only is Richie a top-achieving engineer, he's always looking to find ways to achieve even more.

"It's what drives me," Richie said. "I'm just never satisfied. I don't know where it comes from … sometimes it drives me kind of crazy … but that's how I live my life."

Is Richard Parker really all that *different*? Perhaps he is in a physical sense—at least in terms of what he cannot do with his upper body. However, the kind of passion he displayed early on for bicycles and automobiles is the kind of true desire that anyone can easily recognize in a top performer. Richie has turned naysayers into believers by believing in himself and focusing on staying committed, remaining passionate, and finding creative solutions to any obstacles.

Connecting Concepts

Richie found ways that he, in his own particular way, could realize his dreams. He never really cared what people thought about his physical limitations. Rather, Richie cared about finding a way to accomplish his goals, and he continues to improve at everything he does.

Richie lives the spirit of the Lion (Life-giving Individualization Obstructs Naysayers). He has applied the intelligence, energy, and creative thinking needed to find his own path, silencing all the naysayers while living his dreams.

MOOSE

Market Orientation Obviates Special Empathy

Deep in the kind heart
is love and boundless insight,
while dead hearts stay blind.

I n a faraway kingdom lived a salesman. This salesman was highly confident in his ability to sell his product. Unfortunately, this salesman used the same song and dance each time: an old, poorly designed PowerPoint presentation filled with piles of market data. Best of all, every one of his charts went up and to the right!

The salesman did close some deals using this presentation but, sadly, he was not successful in all corners of the kingdom. Bound and determined, the salesman decided to take a shot at selling to the most important man in the land: the King.

Once granted an audience with the King, the salesman began. "My product is fantastic! Not only that, but I can prove it to you with this presentation." And so began the PowerPoint filled with loads of data, numbers, market graphs, charts, and return-on-investment figures.

At the end, although half of the royal court had fallen asleep, the salesman was still quite confident. Switching off his projector, he asked the King, "Well, sir...what did you think? How many can I put you down for?"

The King leaned back in his throne. "My dear subject, at first I thought you would do wonderfully." His eyes narrowed with disdain.

"But as you carried on, I wanted to kill your product. By the time we got to slide 28 and your ridiculous market segmentation, this presentation had become criminal!" He turned to his guards and shouted, "Off with his head!"

Connecting Concepts

So, the King was no fan of PowerPoint presentations and boring meetings. But the essence of the salesman's flaw was his attachment to general market data rather a true, deep understanding of his customers. The salesman was missing this key: products sell to people, not to generic, misunderstood, vague "market segments" highlighted in charts.

Down with cookie-cutter market data and up with insights, customer empathy, and a true understanding of the value delivered to your prospective customers.

Innovation

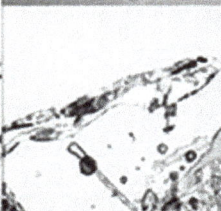
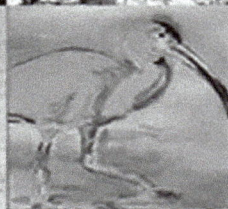
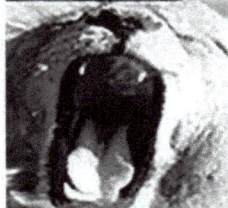

Animals

NENE

Nimble Energetic Nonpareil Employees

Customer pain waits.
the passion to solve trumps all;
genius awakens.

It was the early 1920s, and Minnesota Mining and Manufacturing Company employee Dick Drew was hard at work again. Drew was known as a talented scientist who routinely solved difficult customer problems.

Drew was working on a new type of sandpaper for the company—better known today as 3M—and wanted to see how the new batch would perform in the field. He decided to drive to an auto body shop in St. Paul, Minnesota, to run a test.

Drew walked into the garage and heard fairly typical body shop sounds: the clanking of hammers and loud cursing. Drew asked what the guys were working on. Turns out, two-toned paint jobs were the fad of the day, and to achieve a two-toned effect, the auto painters needed to mask certain parts of the car exterior. They used what was available: heavy adhesive and butcher paper.

However, when the paint dried and the workers peeled off the adhesive tape, quite often, part of the paint layer also peeled away. Hours of hard work were ruined, cursing ensued, and the overall cost to the customer went sky-high. Needless to say, customers were not happy.

Drew watched as the workers did the usual with messed-up two-tone jobs: They sanded everything down and retouched the paint. But

Drew was more of a scientist than a businessman, and he resisted seeing this as an opportunity to sell more sandpaper. Drew was creative, a broad-minded problem-solver. In a flash of inspiration, he saw another way.

What if the adhesive were less aggressive and the paper could peel right off? Drew realized that 3M was already well poised to design and engineer these types of materials. Sandpaper used paper as a backing (obviously!), and a new combination of adhesive and paper could be the genesis of a new type of product: adhesive tape.

Drew went back to the lab with his idea. He tried and tried to get the materials just right to match his vision of adhesive tape, but he couldn't make it work. Frustration reigned.[1]

The president of the company, William McKnight, came by and told him to stop his experiments. "Get back to improving sandpaper," he said. Drew agreed … at first. His detente lasted just one day, then he went back to trying to solve the problem. He immersed himself with renewed enthusiasm and no concern for McKnight's direction.

One day, Drew was right in the middle of an experiment when the door opened and McKnight entered the lab. He looked at Drew, noted the experiment, and kept on walking.

Finally, Drew hit on the right combination of materials and asked McKnight to approve funding for a paper-making machine. Without this rather expensive machine, Drew's dream was dead. McKnight considered the proposal but said no. Drew would not give up, however. As a 3M researcher, he had spending authority for purchases up to $100. So, in a clever move that 3M had not previously seen, he began writing a large stack of $99 purchase orders to pay for the machine.

(Much later, when showing McKnight the machine, he confessed to his scheme. There's no record of McKnight's reaction, except that Drew was certainly not fired. He continued to work for 3M for years.)

The final result of Drew's daring and creative project? The ubiquitous product we now know as "masking tape."

The non-argument between McKnight and Drew in the lab, followed by Drew's openly creative insubordination strategy, have shaped the ethos of 3M's research operations ever since. Together, Drew and McKnight established a new working model for managers and creative workers: If you have the right person on a project they are passionate about, and they are learning fast and staying committed, then get the heck out of the way and let them find the path to success![2]

Connecting Concepts

The innovative company needs to tolerate employee's initiative and trust them. The Nene knows that the engaged, self-directed, passionate employee who can be trusted can move mountains.

OWL

Off-time's Well-known Liberty

As breaks deliver
beyond all expectations,
magic emanates.

When designer Stefan Sagmeister describes the first time he took a sabbatical, he admits that his plan—or rather, his lack of one—was flawed. But over the course of a year, Sagmeister discovered what some of the most successful leaders in the world have known for decades: Time away from work can actually pay off for both workers and their employers, especially when you consider the long-term benefits. Here's how Sagmeister describes it:

"I run a design studio in New York. Every seven years, I close it for one year to pursue some little experiments, things that are always difficult to accomplish during the regular working year. In that year, we are not available for any of our clients. We are totally closed. And, as you can imagine, it is a lovely and very energetic time."

Sagmeister said he is convinced that this refresh period—and the attention he pays to the need for time-off and a change of pace—are critical factors in the success of his top-notch, highly sought-after design work.

Henry Ford is well known for having observed and acted on this phenomenon in his auto manufacturing plants in the 1920s, ultimately reducing his employees' workweek from six days to five. This businessman realized that workers' productivity began to *decrease* once they worked beyond about 40 hours in a one-week period. In addition, their attention to detail began to diminish and they made more mistakes. It just didn't pay for people to be in the factory too long. By simply mandating fewer hours, Ford improved his own bottom line as well as the lives of workers for generations to come.

But back to Sagmeister: While most people would obviously have a hard time pulling off a one-year sabbatical every seven years, researchers are finding that short, frequent breaks can be just as effective at improving efficiency and increasing productivity. A 1999 study by Cornell University's Ergonomics Research Laboratory revealed that staffers who were reminded to take breaks were some 13-percent more accurate in their work than those who were not reminded.

More recent studies have examined the impact on employee productivity of using web surfing to take breaks. On the one hand, it's no secret that workers can waste a lot of time on the Internet. However, the National University of Singapore discovered that those who go online for limited, short periods actually *outperform* their peers who don't go online at all. To be precise, they were *9-percent more productive overall* according to the study's authors.

Sagmeister isn't surprised by any of this. In his talk to TED audiences in October 2009, the noted designer made his case for taking a break.

"What came out of the sabbatical? I really got close to design again. I had fun. Financially, seen over the long term, it was actually successful. Because of the improved quality, we could ask for higher prices," he explained.

He also pointed out the possibility that a company's success could be related to the amount of time employees are afforded to pursue outside interests. He mentioned that both 3M and Google—firms that are "more successful than mine," he admitted—have given workers "flextime" or "unstructured time" for exploring non-work pursuits. This strategy appears to have paid off, as Sagmeister notes. The development of both Scotch Tape and Post-its has been attributed to this freedom for workers. And when Marissa Mayer was a Google executive, she claimed in an interview that 50 percent of the company's new ideas were generated during employee's "20-percent time" (flextime).

There are surely those who will have a hard time accepting that working less can produce better results in both quality and quantity, but as companies continue to compete for the best employees with perks such as unstructured time, sabbaticals, and flextime, it's likely that we'll see this trend more and more. After all, when the upshot is beneficial to everyone involved, it's hard to argue against it.

Connecting Concepts

We know the Owl to be mature and wise. From this wisdom comes a commitment to the most powerful techniques for improving your creativity, productivity, and innovation prowess.

By following the Owl's advice and utilizing well-framed, unstructured time—taken as small creativity sabbaticals or longer, aggregated blocks of time—you will reconnect to your passions, flash-charge your batteries, and increase your effectiveness.

PIG

Perseverance Inspires Growth

The uphill struggle,
always there to separate
success from failure.

There is no such thing as overnight success. Behind every great business and every great business person, there is hard work, dedication, and perseverance.

This doesn't mean that the most successful business people always have great ideas and never make mistakes—far from it. In fact, the story of Brian Chesky—the founder and CEO of popular accommodation booking website Airbnb—shows how even though we often make mistakes, perseverance through those mistakes will ultimately bring you success in business.

As a recent college graduate, Chesky was flat broke and intent on getting himself a "proper job." It was only when one of his friends persuaded him to collaborate on a startup that he really considered setting up a business of his own. Knowing that you want to start a business is one thing, but creating a business idea that has true potential is quite another.

It was at Rhode Island Art School that Chesky and his colleague were taught to find creative solutions to problems. When they realized they couldn't make their rent, they applied a creative solution to the problem, and this would become the foundation of Airbnb.

An international design conference was being hosted in their town, and since all of the hotels were booked up, they were able to subsidize their rent by renting out an airbed in their flat to people who needed accommodation at the conference.

In this simple solution, Chesky had the bones of Airbnb, but it would take a lot of knocks and a lot of learning to build it into the successful web enterprise it is today. Along the way, Chesky would realize things such as how he was limiting the business' success by confining it to accommodation for conferences. He later realized—through an encounter with Barry Manilow's drummer—that it would make sense to allow people to lease their entire house and not just airbeds in a single room. Through these lessons, Chesky and his partner developed their business idea into something that could be scalable with huge potential for growth.

With a lot of time on their hands, Chesky and his business partner experimented with PR campaigns that involved sending out Obama- and McCain-themed breakfast cereals to homeowners who were using Airbnb to provide accommodations for a political rally in Denver. They also pitched a story about Airbnb to local bloggers, and while they got some traction, this plan did not necessarily result in web traffic or conversions.

Now drowning in credit card debt, Chesky was introduced to Y Combinator, the funding source that enabled him to get Airbnb back on track.

He shifted his focus: he completely zeroed in on profitability and gave himself a deadline to achieve it. With a new focus that didn't center on cereal boxes or bloggers, he was able to apply himself and achieve his goals—an achievement made possible only because of the lessons he'd learned along the rocky road to success.

From this point, Airbnb grew at an astounding rate. The site attracts all kinds of visitors from 86 countries across the world, and it helps rent out unique living spaces such as boats and castles.

Chesky was once a guy who had his arm twisted into starting a business, but through perseverance, he is now the founder and CEO of one of the most successful travel startups of the 21st century.

Connecting Concepts

The Pig (Perseverance Inspires Growth) knows about perseverance and the rewards it brings. Without perseverance—and the passion to succeed that fuels it—innovators stall out. An innovator like Chesky, willing to quickly experiment with everything from breakfast cereals to flying cross-country to show up at a prospect's doorstep, have the passion, commitment, and perseverance to find the path to entrepreneurial success.

Innovation

Animals

QUILLPIG

Quiet Understanding and Introspection Lead to Leverageable Passion In a Group

Finding the purpose, matching with applied passion, transforming lives now!

Paul's friend Jeff had been going through a tough time. Both were executives at Proctor and Gamble (P&G), and Jeff had recently taken a new executive position in the paper products area.

Paul, as a respected leader in Marketing Communications, was the kind of executive on whom coworkers leaned for advice in leadership and career navigation. And Paul could tell something was up with his friend Jeff.

Although he was happy with the promotion, Jeff had the feeling that it was possibly the wrong job for him. It was a tough situation considering that at P&G, brand division leaders may not always have had much personal experience with their own product lines when they are tasked with their leadership positions. For example, in Jeff's case, he was now in charge of paper products such as diapers and paper towels— items that, as a consumer, he may not have really paid much attention to.

Well ... let's be blunt about it: Not everyone can be passionate about paper towels. However, after a number of weeks, Paul reconnected with Jeff and noticed that something had dramatically changed Jeff's outlook.

Paul recounts the story of what happened in his must-read book, *Lead with a Story*: [1]

"At the end of a weeklong business trip to Budapest, Hungary, Jeff had a short train ride to the airport for his return home. He sat next to a fellow American now living in Budapest, so they struck up a conversation. When she found out it was his first trip to Hungary, she asked him what he thought of it. In a very cordial manner, he replied that he liked it very much and that there was much to do in Budapest. After finishing the socially graceful answer, however, he began to tell her a little more about what he really thought.

"'The people were very nice,' he said, 'but they all seemed a bit melancholy. Depressed even. And the weather was beautiful, so that wasn't the problem. Most of them just seemed irritable and unhappy.'

"He went on to describe in detail the behavior he saw that led him to his dreary conclusion. As he did, the woman nodded and smiled knowingly, as if to agree with his assessment. When he finished his story, the woman turned quietly and looked out the window in a contemplative manner. After a long pause, and without even looking back at him, she sighed and said matter-of-factly, 'I think it's the toilet paper.'" [Smith 2012]

This may come across simply as a funny story, just a random remark from a fellow American on a train, but nothing could be further from the truth. Toilet paper may be an important yet ultimately mundane part of people's daily lives. However, imagine what your day would be like if you had to use the thinnest, roughest, cheapest toilet tissue on those most delicate of areas. But this was the status of toilet paper in Budapest 15 years ago. If that's all you had ever used, you might be constantly chafed and slightly irritated in your nether regions, too.

Jeff thought, *Perhaps they don't think about toilet paper constantly but enough that every day is a little less pleasant. And that might make you a little short-tempered with a visiting businessman from the States as well as anyone else who crossed your path.* The implication for Jeff's new job was now clear: P&G may not be curing cancer but what they do matters to people probably more than he realized, perhaps even more than anyone realized. "One of my prejudicial notions had just evaporated," he said.

Jeff found the link from job to purpose. He reframed his thinking to optimize himself for passion and purpose.

Are you surprised to hear that Jeff became highly successful running P&Gs paper brands? I didn't think so. The passionate, fully engaged employee—one whose tie-in to purpose is crystal clear—will of course be a focused winner who delights customers. Every time.

Tapping into the essence of innovative productivity is the secret to a hyper-energized leader who makes people say, "That person is cranking out 20 times more than everyone around him!"

Connecting Concepts

The Quillpig sports many pointed quills that aim in different directions. Each point can be thought of as an area of focus. That's not much of a stretch for those of us who are trained to prioritize, focus, and produce key results.

Yet, no one should try to use every single quill— each "point." Instead, how about reframing our passion, choosing the one quill that points to the most powerful direction for you?

This individualized "passion reframe," done in a highly focused manner, is the essence of the Quillpig's innovation power.

Jeff's new passion frame was simple yet unexpected: Quality paper products can make a huge difference not only for individuals but perhaps for a whole nation! This was not merely an insight about paper products … this frame, for Jeff, became an honest-to-God battle cry!

Study the Quillpig along with his quills, and do whatever it takes to reframe for passion so that your quill-focus may be realized. Select the right quill, and almost instantly you become the driver of a passion project where, like others who have successfully framed for passion, you are executing at 10 or 20 times above average.

RAT

Radically Autonomous Team

*To each his own strengths,
pushing bars high from below,
with true conviction.*

The year is 2214. New employees line up outside the front photon door. They walk into the lobby and lasers flash, capturing their DNA and pupil identification tattoos as they walk through the lobby.

Their UWW (Universe-wide Web) ocular implants display the top-secret employee handbook. The handbook has a special section for alien cafeterias and bathroom amenities—broad, intergalactic anatomical diversity is supported by the company as well.

More important, the handbook basically says that, as a new employee, just figure out what you want to do. If you are passionate about something, then it is good and important enough—by definition—so just pull up a mobile desk somewhere and go to it.

The organization is flat: there are no bosses, so work with peers of your choosing. Get your work group together, or join existing one, and just figure out a way to delight customers.

OK ... forget the ridiculous lasers, ID tattoos and bathroom jokes, but realize this: Something very much like this sort of crazy employee on-boarding already exists!

Right now in 2014, at Valve Software Inc., a game development company in Bellevue, Washington, new employees are given a handbook that essentially says, "You figure out what you want to work on, find others to work on it, and just make it happen!"

With the publication of the employee handbook for Valve, a radical new approach to company organization is starting to create waves among those who aren't afraid to experiment and who trust their employees to make the right decisions for both the company and themselves.

At Valve, employees really are given the independence to decide which projects they should be working on and in what capacity they will be most useful. They are empowered to make decisions that can affect every aspect of the business, and there is not one single "boss" in the place. Every team member has the same level of rights and responsibilities as the rest. It's the sort of freedom that would make the CEO of a traditional, hierarchical corporation shudder with fear.

Valve was created in 1996 as the brainchild of founders Gabe Newell and Mike Harrington, both former employees of Microsoft. The company made a splash with the release of its first game, *Half-Life*, in 1998. It has since expanded to develop software and platforms to improve the gaming experience from a variety of different perspectives.

Valve describes itself as an "entertainment studio" to allow for diversification in virtually any way it sees fit. This broadminded approach to the company's development is applied to its employment principles as well. The firm's handbook for new employees makes it explicitly clear that no one's role is set in stone, and job descriptions are fluid, created through self-determination and the motivation to make customers happy by making amazing products.

So far, the strategy seems to be a successful one, with the company's profitability per employee increasing: a good sign that putting their trust in the people they've hired is paying off.

The radical-autonomy approach is an all-encompassing one that goes deeper than simply encouraging employees to do whatever they want. It attempts to develop a workplace where people are happy and satisfied with their jobs. It places heavy emphasis on recruiting and hiring the right people for this type of environment, and it recognizes that it's not the right fit for everyone.

Radical autonomy requires people who are passionate and motivated to create new products and improve existing ones in an effort to delight customers. Obviously, if you hire smart, creative, and competent people, logic follows that they aren't likely to lead your organization into unfixable fiascoes. They can and should be trusted to do their work and make decisions that are in the best interests of their employer and themselves.

This trust can and will result in some risk of failure, and the radical autonomy methodology does not assume that mistakes won't be made. In fact, it anticipates errors because it's asking people to be original and forward-thinking. Employees can rest assured that they won't be fired for a screw-up. Instead, they understand that the only surefire way to avoid mistakes is to stubbornly adhere to tried-and-true thinking that avoids any hint of risk or creativity. This is precisely counter to the environment that Valve hopes to create. Staff are empowered to ask questions, make mistakes, and take responsibility for every aspect of the business.

Described as "Flatland" in the handbook, Valve shuns the old-school hierarchy model of traditional business management. Even Gabe Newell, the remaining founder and president of the company, is fundamentally on the same level as the newest hire in the firm. While there's a healthy respect for those with experience, and newbies are encouraged to ask for advice and help from their coworkers, there isn't a manager or supervisor anywhere to be found. Project teams may appear to have "team leaders," but they serve more as organizational clearinghouses for information and resources rather than bosses. This level playing field leaves everyone more comfortable with pursuing ideas that may have been nixed by a higher-up in a conventional management setting.

Ultimately, this extreme version of self-management appears to be working well for the small startup out of Bellevue, which has grown to more than one hundred employees and is poised for more growth in the near future. As the idea catches on, only time will tell what's possible when entrepreneurs show an interest in discovering the creative powers they can unleash in their employees by simply releasing the reins.

Connecting Concepts

Radically autonomous teams (Rats, if you will) can enable employees to play to their strengths and pursue their passions while doing the best work of their lives. Maybe every company on the planet isn't ready for the Rat right now, but the sheer power of radical autonomy is sure to be a trend that helps more and more companies become stronger creative forces as they evolve their innovation cultures.

SEAL

Seeking Empathy Amplifies Leadership

Looking beneath the surface for new perspectives, unlocking results.

You've all worked for, or with, that bullheaded son of a gun who lays down the law: "My way or the highway."

This leadership approach may have worked in the days of driving rivets into widgets on the assembly line, and it works now with Marine recruits at boot camp, but it sure won't work with highly skilled, creative knowledge workers.

And, when it comes to fast-growth, innovative businesses, who *isn't* a knowledge worker?

By adopting a style of leadership with empathy at its core, would you sacrifice your power in the boardroom? Absolutely not.

Leaders who can formulate strategy, motivate employees to be their best, and steer campaigns with authority do not have to stop empathizing and understanding everyone around them.

But how can you actually be an empathetic leader day to day? Very simply, you take time to listen to your employees, ask for their opinions and points of view, and then listen some more. This will help you achieve what author Daniel Pink calls "attunement": the ability to deeply understand another's point of view by actually "taking their perspective."[1]

Most people are, perhaps unsurprisingly, very skilled at listening to people and asking questions. We all do some amount of this in our daily lives. But because most people believe that effective leadership is one of "command and control," those skills can get pushed to the side, and effectiveness as business leaders is diminished as a result.

By listening to your employees and colleagues, and by asking them questions, you clearly communicate that their point of view is valuable to the business. And of course, that should be the case, otherwise they wouldn't be there, right?

Transformative ideas can come from many different places. The notion that those "big ideas" must be dictated from the top is long gone. The old adage of "two heads are better than one" still rings true and ties in perfectly with the ethos of empathetic leadership. Only by listening to those around you, and by truly trying to understand their thought processes and points of view, can effective collaboration take place.

Empathy and openness may not appear directly related to doing business. This is why you should remember that empathy and openness generate new ideas and drive employee satisfaction. This will ultimately provide a competitive advantage, and that a competitive advantage has a direct effect on the bottom-line.

Connecting Concepts

The Seal has a strong sense of environment, empathizing and coexisting well with the animals around it.

Fast, playful, strategic, and magnificently agile, the seal exemplifies winning leadership. The seal is a powerful innovation animal: Find, observe and emulate the seal.

Innovation

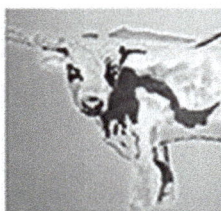

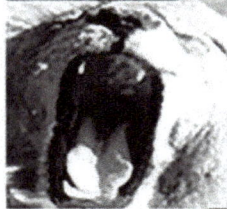

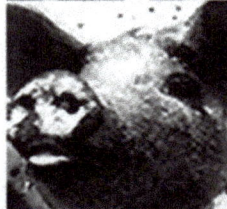

Animals

TIGER

Total Immersion Generates Exceptional Results

Deep, deep commitment,
dedication beyond norms,
garnering success.

Utter commitment to a vision sounds compelling, even sexy. Few things in life inspire such admiration as the dedication and commitment needed to totally immerse yourself, and a whole team, into pursuing a big, scary, hairy stretch goal.

As a relevant example, few stand out like Apple's iPhone.

By any normal measure, the plan to build the iPhone—and therefore revolutionize the ubiquitous cell phone—was a clear impossibility. When Apple looked at the manufacturing costs of its ambitious project, most normal people would have panicked. Could they even manufacture this solid aluminum, art-house sculpture? Or would the whole company just tank?

As it turns out, Apple was quite comfortable diving headfirst into the chilly waters of innovation-driven unknowns.

Enter Jony Ive.

Ive, Apple's head of design and chief confidante of CEO Steve Jobs, was the driving force behind the company's breakthroughs in industrial design. The iPhone—following the enormously successful Mac and iPod designs, which had energized consumers and changed the world of computer products—was going to be even more beautiful, functional, and outrageous as its predecessors.

Ive oversaw the iPhone from paper sketch to the final aluminum casing, milled perfectly to the micron. To achieve this never-before-attempted design, Apple scoured the planet to buy up every half-million-dollar Computer Numerical Control (CNC) machine they could find.

These machines had never been used for mass manufacturing but only for small runs of precision-milled prototypes. The idea of using them to mass-produce the new iPhone was—to say the least—a bit nuts.

But Ive was committed. He and the design team wanted to make devices that had tighter tolerances, fit together more smoothly, and were more attractive, lightweight, and robust than any other devices out there. Already, Macs and iPods stood in stark contrast to the brittle, bulky plastic of competitors' computers and music players.

Ive's experience with a wide range of materials, from wood to metal to glass, factored in heavily to take the iPhone design to a whole new level never before seen in the industry. Design, beauty, and usability would not be compromised. So, when it came to actually building the iPhone, they were 3D-printed and carved on CNC machines in the Apple design studio. Nothing less would do.

And you already know the rest of the story.

The innovation lessons are clear: Stick with your world-changing vision; go ahead and do things that don't scale. Heck, do things that don't even make sense. At first. Then when you do figure out a way to scale your vision, you have a unique advantage, a durable breakthrough that opens up a world of possibilities.

Micro-machining consumer devices as gorgeous works of art, milled to perfection out of light, strong aluminum was about the least scalable approach imaginable. But Apple—and Ive—stared impossibility in the face and just made things happen.

The approach did cost money. But success talks … loudly. The amazing example Apple was setting had more to do with risk tolerance, courage, and commitment and less to do with the particulars of cost. In the innovation game, creative breakthroughs that produce an awesome product seriously trump even the best possible cost control measures.

Connecting Concepts

If you forge the course and have the guts to dent the universe, then many billions could come your way.

The Tiger drives this type of success. Runaway success demands complete, absolute immersion in the vision of innovation. At Apple, the tradition of design, the "insanely great" attitude, and the reality distortion field floating about are the pathos of the Tiger. Embrace the Tiger, be bold, and don't hold back anything.

URIAL

Under-Represented Individual As Lead User

Solving for the one true target; a life we will together transform.

Is creating new products to delight and awe customers an art or a science?

The question is old enough and complex enough to challenge most experts in the field of innovation. That is, except perhaps Steve Blank and Eric Von Hippel.

Steve Blank, known as father of the Lean Startup movement and creator of the "customer development" methodology, and Eric Von Hippel, who has pioneered the concepts of democratized innovation and the "lead user" concept, have developed concepts that, when combined, provide us with a revolutionary idea:

Out there in the world are some special users who care more about, and will teach you more about, your product innovation than anyone else in the world. And you don't need to find many of them!

Blank and Von Hippel recognized that the earliest buyers of a product or service could be the most important to its overall growth. They determined that these customers—the *lead users*—could also be crucial in determining the final product for a wider market.

Lead users are a special lot: They need a new product or service and are searching for something to meet that need. These lead users know exactly what they need, what they like to use and, just as important, what they are willing to pay.

Some people have a problem with this. They say, "Wait. If I select only a few customers and go deep with them, then I will end up with a product only a few people even like." You might call this "fear of the long-tailed person": the assumption that lead users have nothing in common with the rest of the human race.

However, this is almost never the case and therefore is an irrational fear. You can use your judgment in selecting lead users. Working with the few customers who are the bulls-eye on your target will do more good than connecting with a million of the wrong people. There is plenty of time to reach millions later, once you have validated your path.

By determining the *actual* needs of users through observation and experimentation—rather than trying to guess or waste time solving problems that aren't that important to people—the business can focus its efforts on solving the issue at hand.

This kind of interaction with the customer also gives the company a chance to base their prices on what their product or service is *worth* to the customer rather than strictly on production costs. A startup may be able to increase their price if lead users place a high value on the product or service, or they may discover that they need to look for ways to decrease costs if the value is considered to be low. Either way, the earlier in the game this sort of information is gained, the better.

What's more, first customers often become a company's biggest cheerleaders. Referred to as "customer-evangelists," these people model a product or service for the rest of the world, making it accessible and desired. They are the ones who introduce your company to the larger market, and their word-of-mouth can undoubtedly make or break a new business.

Connecting Concepts

We all know that innovators must be brave enough to explore new products and services. The Urial, a wild, bearded sheep, stands out there in unusual territory, hooves dug into the edges of cliffs overlooking the vast and jagged canyons of opportunity. The Urial is out in the lead, seeing things other animals don't see, creating a deep, valuable, and unique perspective that few think to mine.

The Urial embodies the spirit of our lead users, a wonderful resource for innovators of all types. Study the Urial; this innovation animals stands on the edge of the new and old, and it brings a wealth of knowledge to those brave enough to accept it.

Innovation

Animals

VIPER

Very Important Prioritized Experiments Rule

*One thousand attempts
to solve, each wrong, failing quickly;
now we see the way.*

Thomas Edison tested more than 1,600 materials to find the right filament for the light bulb. His test materials included coconut fiber and fishing line, not to mention hairs from a friend's beard. Now that is commitment to experimentation!

The Toyota Motor Company is similarly committed. Toyota recently experimented with navigation system innovations. Did this multi-billion-dollar-a-year world leader go out and hire the top consultants, paying millions to run exhaustive market tests?

Not at all.

They slapped an off-the-shelf Android tablet into a car's dash, coded up a special app that narrowly tested a "better navigation" hypothesis, and recruited users off Craig's List to try out the new navigation system. Minimizing time per experiment was their goal, and their rapid experimentation gave them more information in just a month than they could have gleaned by spending $5 million over three years in old-school market research.

At Intuit, a channel sales team decided to try out an idea, one they had been discussing on and off around the coffee pot and water cooler for a year. In just one afternoon, they ran an experiment to try out a different phone script for end-users calling for help with QuickBooks.

The new script quickly showed that it helped customers better by getting them the right solution, and two hours later, the initially underwhelmed sales manager came back and said, "Yep! Your data shows this will probably add about $2 million in revenue a year. Good two hours, work team!"

Turns out she was wrong—the revenue uptick is looking more like *$5 million a year and climbing.*

At Steve Blank's Lean Entrepreneurism class at Stanford University, a team developing a crop-picking robot told him that given the minimum viable product (MVP) needed to run meaningful experiments, the robot would take about six months to build.

"It needs image recognition, AI, and the latest algorithm for image-navigation robotics from the Electrical Engineering Department," they said.

Steve said, "I want to see the MVP built by next Thursday, or I will show you this thing you've never seen before in your academic lives: the letter 'C.'"

Few Stanford students had ever seen a "C" grade but had heard of its existence, so they heeded the warning. Five days later, the team came back with a functional MVP: a camera and a computer strapped to the top of a wooden wagon.

"We figured out that the real leap of faith was around the machine's harvesting in real time," they said. "We could pre-bake the data, essentially faking the artificial intelligence part on the back-end, and still test the most important thing quickly."

Steve smiled. That was the way to get an "A" and rapidly experiment. Six months later, the team barely remembered this first early struggle over MVP design in Professor Blank's class because they were really busy as a robotic agriculture startup company funded by venture capitalists.

Connecting Concepts

In the world of new-school entrepreneurism as outlined in Eric Ries' *Lean Startup*, a team's speed through the build-test-learn loop is the most important metric of all. Of course, you have to have the right "leap of faith" hypothesis: the thing that has to be true for your idea to work. Framing the hypothesis as a numerical outcome—"If X is successful, then Y numerical outcome will happen"—is very useful.

An organization whose teams use carefully prioritized experiments is the ultimate learning organization. As small teams pursue learning through rapid experimentation, this method it becomes the norm. An organization can then transform its innovation culture into a meritocracy, one based on the currency of experimentally validated customer learning rather than the currency of pretty PowerPoints and precisely-pitched HiPPO ideas.

Here in the world of prioritized lean experimentation, anyone can be a successful innovator—anyone, that is, who is an empathetic, diligent, rapid experimenter.

Our Viper models such scientific entrepreneurism. With no legs or any other biologically expensive appendages, the viper makes do, moving quickly, quietly, in a serenely intense manner while winding to the manifest destination with style and vigor.

Note the Viper, an animal worthy of respect.

WHALE

Wise Hypotheses Actualize Liberating Experimentation

*Below then above,
the whale's bold strength, matches with
clear intelligence.*

When advanced business strategies are the topic, what comes to mind for you?

For me, I think of "underpants gnomes." No, really.

It all started watching Max Levchin, co-founder of PayPal and successful serial entrepreneur, talk to the crowd at Y-Combinator's startup school.

When Max Levchin talks, people listen. There are about a billion reasons (as in bucks) to listen to Max.

Max, T-shirt-adorned and fired up as usual, took the podium and told the crowd about one of his favorite startup and business strategy lessons. The lesson comes from the "Underpants Gnomes" episode of the TV show *South Park*. I suspect you won't see this show's lessons presented at the Harvard School of Business or the London School of Economics—but perhaps you should.

Here's what the "underpants gnomes" are all about:

The little round-headed kids from South Park are about to give a presentation to town voters. The boys explain why the town should prevent a big, scary corporation ("Harbucks") from opening next door to Tweek's Coffee, a friendly establishment with strong roots in the community. The boys run into a group of gnomes who have been stealing underpants as part of a big plan. The gnomes have a three-phase plan that goes like this:

- Phase 1: Collect Underpants
- Phase 2: ???
- Phase 3: Profit

The South Park boys question the gnomes, asking how exactly they go from collecting underpants to profit. The gnomes do not have any answer.

Sound ridiculous? If only this episode weren't so true to life! The lesson of the underpants gnomes is a lesson worth repeating. It works the same way with a lot of businesses. The business point of view often goes like this:

- Phase 1: Declare a big, bold, compelling vision, complete with pretty PowerPoint slides, which gets you funding and enthusiastic support.
- Phase 2: ???.
- Phase 3: Amazing, over-the-top fame and billions of dollars.

Yet, entrepreneurism and business strategy should really be the art of figuring out what happens in Phase 2 and determining whether that will lead to the desired outcome. Phase 2, rather than being the giant blank of wishful thinking, should in fact be the passion, perseverance, and secret sauce to business success.

Given that most businesses start with one strategy but need to adjust and pivot as they learn the path to success, having a series of question marks in phase 2 is the kiss of death.

Connecting Concepts

Enter our friend the Whale …

Business success is all about hypotheses, experimentation, learning, and converting the search for business success into a workable, scalable business model.[1]

As Eric Reis of Lean Startup fame said, the fast, two-minute montage in the middle of movies—the part where all the useful work actually gets done—is virtually skipped over in movies because it's so dull to watch. All that Phase-2 work is no fun for anyone to watch or, in some cases, even think about.

As Steve Blank said, "We've had *product* development organizations for centuries, but everyone wants to just ignore *customer* development. It is much more fun to just think the magic will happen, just build it and they will come, and that our first-slot thoughts and assumptions will obviously result in throngs of delighted customers." Instead, Blank said, "Get outside the building, find the truth. Inside the building there are just opinions …."

So what should Phase 2 be all about? The Whale, of course. Even though wishful thinking has us believe that our initial approach—collecting underpants—will bring us right to the Phase 3 vision, this is not reality. The way to find our path to Phase 3 is to understand our assumptions about how to get there. Then we embark on a process of learning via experimentation.

Even the best business minds of all times—like Steve Jobs for example—would often learn as they went and even made a few U-turns along the way. Although this is not cool and sexy to point out … we'd all rather think about the lone super-genius who has everything set in his mind from the get-go … Steve Jobs would often change direction as needed.

For example, the Apple I computer was not exactly a runaway success. After receiving customer feedback from the BYTE shop, the Apple II came out with the power supply, keyboard, and central processing packaged together in one box.

Similarly, Pixar's first stab at *Toy Story* featured a moody and acerbic cowboy Woody. The team needed to rewrite and reshoot a friendly Woody before one of the most amazing breakthroughs in the history of film was released.

The Whale cautions us to not be underwear gnomes. Rather, the Whale gives us a process to hypothesize, experiment, and move forward while finding the true path.

XEME

Xerox's Management Education

Genius so dormant;
too timid and stilted to
create the future.

When the brand name "Xerox" comes up in conversation, most people do not think of world-changing inventions such as the Internet and personal computers. In most people's minds, "Xerox" is synonymous with photocopiers, whereas just about everything about today's personal computer technology comes from either Apple or Microsoft.

However, most people would be shocked to learn that before we became the "information generation" connected globally through our many glowing screens, Xerox—not Apple or Microsoft—had the future of computing in its labs.

The Golden Goose lived in Xerox's Palo Alto Research Center (PARC) way back in 1973 as the Xerox Alto: a single machine with a screen, a keyboard for input, a mouse, and a graphical interface. Sound familiar? Yet the Alto was developed by a team of brilliant inventors many years before the earliest Mac was a gleam in Steve Jobs' eyes.

The PARC team, put together by Xerox to devise ways that computers could be more useful and convenient, came up with these astonishing technological breakthroughs, not to mention an "inter-network routing system" that transmitted data through Ethernet cables: the precursor to today's Internet.

Why, then, is Xerox not the biggest name in technology today? They had the vision and capability to create incredible, world-changing breakthroughs but they lacked someone with their finger on the pulse of the market—a customer-focused innovation mindset. Xerox' leadership wanted to make better *photocopiers* and, in the process, seriously underestimated the potential of the computer technology they had produced.

Instead of capitalizing on this remarkable technology or even patenting the ideas, Xerox invited up-and-comers in the computer industry—including Bill Gates and Steve Jobs—to see what they were creating at PARC. These two brilliant and incredibly market-savvy men realized the potential in what they were seeing, and Jobs rushed to get his hands on as much of the intellectual property as possible.

The rest, as they say, is history.

Xerox gave away the Golden Goose, selling the idea of a graphical, bit-mapped computer display and mouse-based navigation for a pittance. A few years later, the first Mac was born, and the Goose continues to lay those golden eggs for Apple to this day.

Connecting Concepts

The Xeme is no goose, golden or otherwise. Xerox serves as an example of how a company can invent the future in one division but ultimately not understand what they have accomplished.

Without an overall mechanism for bringing new, experimental technologies to the market, the "labs division" approach in companies may either bury technological treasure or virtually give it all away to the next savvy neighbor who comes strolling down the street.

Remember the Xeme.

Innovation

Animals

YAK

Year-over-year Appreciation, Kindness

Standing on shoulders,
great, strong, committed, loving,
as we now succeed.

Captain Charlie Plumb flew jet fighters off the aircraft carrier *U.S.S. Kitty Hawk* back in the 1960s. One morning, he climbed into his fighter and taxied forward. The yellow shirts hooked him to the catapult, and he was ready to launch off the carrier deck.[1]

It was Captain Plumb's last sortie, ever.

He was shot down and spent six years as a prisoner of war of the Vietcong.

Some years later, while Plumb was eating at a restaurant in Kansas City, a man two tables away kept looking at him. Plumb noticed the man's stare but didn't recognize the gentleman.

The man then walked over to his table, pointed, and said, "You are Captain Plumb!" which he confirmed.

The man then seemed to go into a trance, reciting a story as if he were narrating a fairy tale or legend. He told the story of Plumb's work as a pilot. He told him how he flew jet fighters over Vietnam and that he served aboard the *Kitty Hawk*. The man recounted how Plumb was shot down and parachuted into enemy hands, where he was held as prisoner of war for six years.

"How in the world did you know all that?" Plumb demanded.

"Because," he replied, "I packed your parachute."

Plumb was shocked. He related the moment:

"I staggered to my feet and held out a very grateful hand of thanks.... He grabbed my hand, he pumped my arm and said, 'I guess it worked.' 'Yes sir, indeed it did,' I said, 'and I must tell you I've said a lot of prayers of thanks for your nimble fingers, but I never thought I'd have the opportunity to express my gratitude in person.'"[1]

Parachute packers worked in the bowels of the aircraft carrier. They rarely saw the light of day and worked long hours in hot, humid, cramped conditions. But parachute packers knew that their work kept pilots alive. They were indispensable.

Connecting Concepts

Who are your parachute packers?

The essence of transcendent leadership may lie in appreciation, observation, empathy, judgment, and gratitude. The moments in life when you want to shout and scream, "Good lord, this person is so important to me!" can create peak experiences of gratitude. These moments can be key in a lifetime of accomplishment, success, and teamwork.

The Yak—strong, impressive, quiet, a dedicated worker—exemplifies the essence of dedicated and longitudinal support of others. Without parachute packers—the Yaks of our world—innovators would have no strong, dedicated shoulders on which to stand. They would toil in desolate isolation, subject to the swirling tides of under-supported and scratching progress.

Find the Yak and thank the Yak. Repeatedly. This innovation animal is a lifesaver.

Innovation

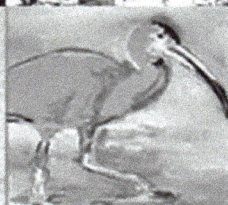

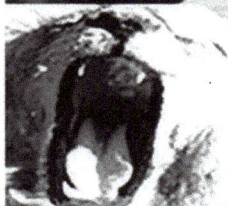

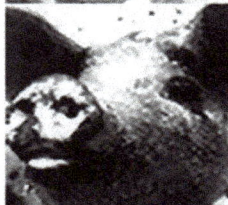

Animals

ZEBRA

Zigzag Exploration Brings Resulting Awesomeness

Behold paths unknown.
such lines defy straightness to
enable greatness.

Eric Ries, author of *The Lean Startup*, stood in front of 400 Intuit employees—that was the number of people who could fit into the large conference room. Thousands of other employees watched live on Intuit TV, itching to get a sense of "WWED" (What would Eric do?) when it came to moving their projects forward in a lean and entrepreneurial manner.

Eric pointed out that one of the most common recent confusions about *The Lean Startup* had to do with the nearly ubiquitous term "pivot." Eric had introduced the term in *The Lean Startup* to denote a change in strategy without a change in vision. [Eric Ries 2010] Now, he joked that "pivot" had become one of the most overused terms in the world of business, and people were want to call almost anything and everything a pivot.

Eric clarified what he really had in mind regarding the value and definition of "pivot": the vision is the target ... where you need to go.

"Let's say we are leaving the Bay Area here on a trip to St Louis. We know where we want to go. This destination doesn't 'pivot'; it is the vision and it doesn't change. Even if we start driving west then decide we need to take the more southern route, so we change directions, we've pivoted on the 'how,' or the idea, but we are still going to St Louis!"

We can see that this model of pivoting applies to many of the greatest product innovations in history. For example:

The Apple I essentially came out wrong. It needed to pivot, to have the power supply and keyboard fully integrated into one friendlier-than-ever personal computer box. This was the Apple II. Sales went ballistic for the Apple II. This put-it-in-one-friendly-package pivot created the personal computer industry.

The Pixar movie *Toy Story* sucked. Well ... I'm talking about the version that was never released. In an earlier version, Woody was a mean cowboy, and the movie just wasn't working, it wasn't fun. The plot needed something different, some kindness, some real buddy-buddy rapport among the leading characters. Pixar stepped back from early tests, thought it over, rewrote Woody (a big pivot) and then released what became a blockbuster. That major script correction changed the course of animated films for good. [1]

Twitter started out as podcasting infrastructure company. But Ev Williams and some other folks decided to jam, spend some time playing around with other ideas. This big pivot swung the "how" all the way from a platform for audio user-contributed content to a microblogging platform. However, you could still say that the vision was people interacting, communicating with new speed and fluency. The path led to one of the biggest social networking breakthroughs in Internet history.

Viagra started as a blood pressure medication. In didn't work too well at reducing blood pressure but it had a very interesting side effect. 'Nuff said. Big pharma took notice, pivoted, and reframed the product. Sadly enough, this eventually resulted in all men receiving amazing volumes of junk email regarding the geometry and stamina of the anatomical components in question. Maybe not the greatest pivot ever.

More common are the thousands of pivots we haven't mentioned where course corrections, based on new insights and customer behavior data, have allowed entrepreneurs to tweak and change their approach to inspire the hearts and minds of previously apathetic end-users. The seemingly small, measured, less-glamorous pivots happening on a daily basis—from web A/B tests to customer interviews to Google analytics-based insights that alter a funnel—are changing the world.

Yes, the term "pivot" climbed way too high, way too fast, up the hype curve. However, the value of the right pivot—done well, based on learning rather than opinion or blind adherence to this-has-to-be-the-plan thinking—is a breakthrough methodology.

Connecting Concepts

The Zebra is all about exploration. The myriad zigzag paths of pivoting strategies to reach a goal is the Zebra's *modus operandi*.

Without pivots and their resulting zigzagged paths of course corrections, ventures would have to be absolutely correct from the get-go or would fail. The Zebra allows, and even encourages, learning and adjusting along the way as you and your organization find the winning path.

Honor the Zebra and, if you can get away with it, *ride* the Zebra.

Appendix A
Putting the Innovation Animals to work

Each of the twenty-six Innovation Animals represents a unique set of innovation concepts. Similarly, Native Americans associated behavioral and philosophical characteristics with each animal in their ecosystem.

The original peoples of the Pacific Northwest used totem poles: carvings of animal forms as a way of retelling an event or communicating the philosophical example associated with an animal's form. Often, tribes assigned totems to families and individuals, with each element of the totem representing the spirit of one animal. Totems often consisted of nine animals, all stacked in a wood sculpture, to tell the story and carry the spirit of a family or individuals.

Innovation Tool #1: Your Innovation Animal Totems

Start with a short totem of three animals. Choose the animals that resonate most strongly with your talents and interests. For example, mine are the Ape, Rat, and Zebra.

What is your story? What will be your Innovation Animal Totem?

Do you work in a team? Better yet, do you work in a team that plays to your strengths and principles? If you can, have each team member take the <u>Strength Finder</u> exercise and choose their totem animals based on key strengths and interests.[1]

Lessons from the Ape, Rat, Kite and Tiger

> *Think of the Ape as an equation: p*
> *passion = autonomy × purpose × excellence*

Of these three key elements, no value can be zero, or the passion will not be there.

However, don't expect uniformity in the magnitude of each variable. As you work to increase personal as well as overall team passion for any innovative project, do what you can to maximize the value of each variable in the equation.

Innovation Tool #2: Designing for Delight

The Dog exposes us to the power of design thinking. One key design thinker, Herbert Simon, describes design thinking as a seven step process: *Define, Research, Ideate, Prototype, Choose, Implement, Learn.*

Whether Simon's process framework is the ultimately helpful innovation tool or not, it is clear that design thinking propels us far past the arcane "have the big brain folks design a whole solution up front, then put the project on a waterfall schedule" approach of yesteryear. The Simon model implies an on-going cycle of observing, researching thinking, experimenting and learning.

This model embraces the true challenges of successful innovation.

Intuit has taken another approach: the essentials of design thinking were distilled down to a clean, 3 pillar model. These pillars are:

(1) Deep customer empathy,

(2) going broad to then go narrow, and

(3) rapid experimentation.

The company built sets of innovation tools and light processes around these 3 pillars -- which are referred to as 'Design for Delight (D4D)' -- an internal branding of the Design Thinking concepts.[3]

Innovation Tool #3: The Autonomy Audit

Do you feel free to effectively innovate? The autonomy audit, introduced by Dan Pink in his book *Drive*, will help you and team members to assess where they are, how to improve, and how to stay on track.

Read more at Pink's amazing blog: www.danpink.com/yamjam/. You will not be disappointed.

The Autonomy Audit Questionnaire[2]

Ask your team to answer each of the four questions below. The questions should be scored numerically, with 10 being "an enormous amount" and 0 meaning "very little or none at all."

Scores approaching 40 points mean you've reached the autonomy nirvana of "Jonathan Livingston Seagull-level freedom." Scores below 15 mean you are living the workplace equivalent of a Siberian prison work camp.

1. How much autonomy do you have over your tasks at work: your main responsibilities and what you do in a given day?
2. How much autonomy do you have over your time at work: for instance, when you arrive, when you leave, and how you allocate your hours each day?
3. How much autonomy do you have over your team at work: that is,

to what extent are you able to choose the people with whom you typically collaborate?

4. How much autonomy do you have over your technique at work: how you actually perform the main responsibilities of your job?

And now for the mother of all autonomy inquires:

Do you make "Stephen Covey quadrant-two time" for yourself, meaning that you reserve time to think about non-emergency, strategic approaches to improving yourself and your results?

Related to that, do you or your company support "unstructured time"? This can take the form of 20-percent time, 15-percent time, whatever your variation may be. If not, why not? It's good enough for Google, 3M, Intuit, Nike, Atlassian, and a plethora of other premier innovation companies—so why not yours?

Innovation Tool #4: The Excellence Template

Fill in the blanks:

1. **Goal**: My desire is to improve the following

_____.

2. **Focus**: I will improve by working on

_____.

3. **Measurement**: Open loop systems—those with no feedback loop—tend to support the concept of entropy more than the principle of continuous improvement. Therefore, commit to the following credo: "I will measure my progress. I'll know I'm getting better by

_____."

Innovation Tool #5: Your Personal Purpose Sentence

The one short sentence that sums up what I am "about" is this:

_____.

As an example, the one-sentence-purpose I came up with in a jam we held last year was: "I help people tap into their passions so they can shine."

Lessons from the Bull, Pig, and Frog

Innovation Tool #6—Accountability and Empowerment

Answer these key questions about accountability and empowerment:

1. Do you feel fully accountable for the work you do? Do you "own" the results? Why or why not? *Hint, the correct answer is "yes"; otherwise, we really need a chapter on learned helplessness!*
2. How do you influence those around you?
3. How might you make your business (and the lives of those around you) a little better each day?

Do you have fears in each category? How many, and why?

Lessons from the Dog, Ibis, Jaguar, Seal, Zebra, and Giraffe

"Design thinking" emphasizes deep empathy, rapid experimentation and "going broad to go narrow" thinking.[3]

Using an empathy map (figure 2) can help you get to the "why" of customer behavior.

Eric Ries describes the build-measure-learn loop as the essence of lean startups (figure 2). How might you execute frugal experimentation loops in the course of reaching your goals?

Going broad with brainstorming can help you obtain better insights and solutions. Try "brainwriting": This method consists of choosing a trigger question and then using a timed interval—say, three minutes—to write down on a Post-it note each idea that comes to mind.

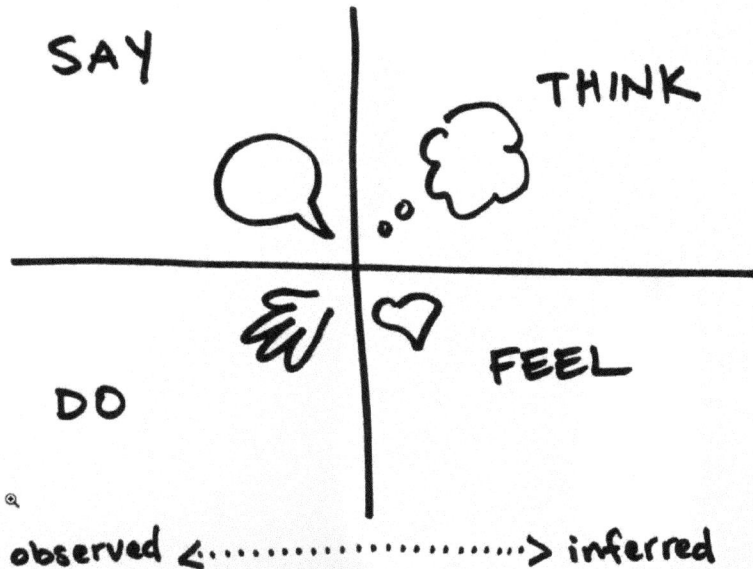

Figure 2[2]

Innovation Tool #7: Courage and Persistence

Here are questions inspired by the Cat:
- What, right this moment, are you avoiding? Let's say the world is full of "good fear" and "bad fear." Good fear is wise and informed, instructing us on proper, strategic action. Bad fear is the essence of timidity and helplessness, emotional states that lead to avoidance, quitting, or at least sub-par execution.
- What is on your "good fear" list? What is on your "bad fear" list? How might you knock that bad fear list down to nothing?

Innovation Tool #8: The Build-measure-learn Lifestyle[4]

Use this rubric to guide your rapid experimentation:
1. When your innovation is complete and heavily in use five years from now, what is a user of your innovation experiencing? Envision the experience.
2. What was the key idea, the essence of your innovation, which got you there? Hold onto this thought but be willing to modify it later. As Amazon CEO Jeff Bezos said, "We are stubborn on vision, flexible on the details." How you "get there," your key idea, is the details part.
3. List all the assumptions you are making about your key idea. Dig deep. Realize you have blind spots and think of five more assumptions than you possibly think you can get to.
4. Select the assumption that is absolutely most crucial to your idea. Which assumptive idea, if proven wrong, would make your idea unworkable? Call this assumption your "leap of faith" assumption.
5. Imagine there is a way to quickly test whether your assumption is right or wrong. Frame the purpose of the test (or experiment) as an if/then statement: "If I do X, then Y will happen." This statement is your hypothesis. Note: It is best if your hypothesis is objectively, even quantitatively, measurable.
6. Write down your experiment. This is the detailed expansion of your if/then hypothesis. What is the fastest, most inexpensive, and most accurate way to execute the experiment?
7. Run the experiment and be BRUTALLY HONEST with yourself about the outcome.
8. What did you learn? Is your idea still workable? If not, consider "pivoting" to a new solution. Write down what you've learned.
9. Given what you've learned, what do you need to learn next? Hint: Repeat steps 3-8, or 2-8 in the pivot case.

The tool above is essentially *The Lean Startup* condensed into an odd, short questionnaire. Purists may call this "lean heresy," so please feel encouraged to read *The Lean Startup* by Eric Ries and *The Startup Owner's Manual* by Steve Blank. These books will equip you to improve your innovation game many fold.

Are you thinking that only eight innovation tools may be a bit light? Me too. Be on the lookout for the *Innovation Animals Workbook*, chock-full of easy-to-use tools for end-to-end innovation, coming out next year!

Epilogue
Being an Innovation Animal

You awake each morning excited to face challenges that lie ahead.

Resistance awaits you—this is expected.

You welcome these struggles, given that worthy accomplishments must always overcome stubborn resistance.

The path ahead is a grit-your-teeth, evolving spiral of building, measuring, and learning. With cunning, you move along a swift yet zigzagging and jagged path, bridging blind spots with rapidly synthesized learning.

Validation is neither your goal nor metric. Rather, you pursue personally obtained truths that defy the diversionary cloak of wishful thinking.

Your journey is habit as evolving déjà vu: Each trail post passed marks an increased depth of empathy, a speedy iteration, and a measure of improvement.

This is your life; therefore you are an Innovation Animal.

More modest than meek, the Innovation Animals may not inherit the earth but they shall make the earth a better place.

Acknowledgements

The truth is, animals don't write books, people do—with lots of help. I'm grateful to all the people who helped so much with this project. I'm particularly grateful for the pod of Kickstarter backers who've made this possible. I want to thank the very generous backers Chuck Eaneff, Amit Jain, Carol and Mike Stanek, Brian McDonnell, Sherry Denton, Catherine Cornelius, and Elizabeth Zias for their kind-hearted and substantial pledges.

Amy Walker Miller was the dream editor who every author should meet. I've been continually surprised by her ability to quickly find un-sanded corners, hanging threads, and ugly prose-contusions that must be healed.

The watercolor artists who made this book so colorful and energizing are B. Sakura, Anca Benera, and T. Reispe—all from Romania. These are wonderful folks I have only met online but are truly talented, global artists. If this is what Al Gore had in mind when he invented the Internet, well then, it is working! I was personally inspired, about twenty-six times, by these artists' talent and dedication.

References and Notes

Chapter Ape:

- CRC Press, "Of Friday Night Experiments and Graphene", posted 7 Jul 2011 23:49 by Liming Leong

Chapter Bull:

- Source Metrics, "United Dave", 2011 [http://blog.sourcemetrics.com/carleton-university-presents-a-d-dunton-award-to-united-breaks-guitars-creator-dave-carroll/]

- [United 2] http://www.fastcompany.com/1320152/broken-guitar-has-united-playing-blues-tune-180-million

Chapter Cat:

- [Aamoth2012] -http://techland.time.com/2012/09/27/google-turns-14-today-was-initially-called-backrub/ - Doug Aamoth @daamoth

- [Time2012Aam] Read more: Google Turns 14, Was Initially Called 'BackRub' | TIME.com http://techland.time.com/2012/09/27/google-turns-14-today-was-initially-called-backrub/#ixzz2laELVf00

- [GrahamBlog2010] - http://www.paulgraham.com/ambitious.html

Chapter Dog:

- "Design Thinking"; Tim Brown … http://www.ideo.com/by-ideo/design-thinking-in-harvard-business-review

- Fast Co article … http://www.fastcompany.com/919258/design-thinking-what

Chapter Elk:

- The Washington Post – "How to completely, utterly destroy an employee's work life"; Teresa Amabile and Steven Kramer; Teresa Amabile is a professor and director of research at Harvard Business School. Steven Kramer is a developmental psychologist and researcher. They are coauthors of *The Progress Principle*.

Chapter Frogs:

- [Brian Tracy 2007] *Eat That Frog!: 21 Great Ways to Stop Procrastinating and Get More Done in Less Time*, 128 pages, Edition: Second, Publisher: Ingram, Date: Jan 2007

- [Edward Hess 2012] http://www.fastcompany.com/1842583/3-ways-successful-people-prioritize-their-do-lists; Grow to Greatness: Smart Growth for Entrepreneurial Business *by Edward D. Hess. (c) 2012 Board of Trustees of the Leland Stanford Jr. University*

Chapter Giraffe:

- [Hansleman2012] AndyHansleman.com;
  http://www.andyhanselman.com/2012/05/18/joshie-the-giraffe-a-remarkable-story-about-customer-delight/

Chapter Hippo:

- http://www.forbes.com/sites/derosetichy/2013/04/15/what-happens-when-a-HiPPO-runs-your-company/

- http://www.cbsnews.com/news/when-highest-paid-persons-opinion-stomps-on-your-project/

Chapter Kite:

- *Nuru International*; Building the world's first self-sustaining, self-scaling, integrated development model to end extreme poverty.

Chapter Lion:

- http://now.msn.com/richie-parker-was-born-without-arms-but-nothing-stops-him

- http://www.christianpost.com/news/man-born-without-hands-is-engineer-for-nascars-most-winning-organization-101675/ told ESPN in a recent interview.

Chapter Nene:

- [Mary Bellis 2012] Mary Bellis   About.com , Richard Drew, and Tape; Inventorshttp://inventors.about.com/od/sstartinventions/a/Scotch_Tape.htm

- [Phil Ament 2007] Phil Ament. *The invention of masking tape*. Troy MI: ©1997-2007 The Great Idea Finder, 2007. Online. Available at http://www.ideafinder.com . Research accessed 2013

Chapter Owl:

- http://www.theatlantic.com/business/archive/2011/08/why-summer-vacations-and-the-internet-make-you-more-productive/244289/

- research: http://baselinescenario.com/2011/09/08/the-importance-of-time-off/

- TED talk: http://www.ted.com/talks/stefan_sagmeister_the_power_of_time_off.html

Chapter Pig:

- Startup School - Brian Chesky - Startup School 2010; http://www.youtube.com/watch?v=ZPLnfUPBXwA;

Chapter Quillpig:

- Smith, Paul (2012-08-08). Lead with a Story: A Guide to Crafting Business

Narratives That Captivate, Convince, and Inspire (Kindle Locations 3202-3210). Amazon - A. Kindle Edition.

Chapter Rat:

- [Shane Snow 2012] Fast Company; http://www.fastcompany.com/1835546/youre-hired-now-figure-things-out-help-whimsical-handbook

- [Steve Denning 2012] Steve Denning, Forbes.com, http://www.forbes.com/sites/stevedenning/2012/04/27/a-glimpse-at-a-workplace-of-the-future-valve/; Contributor, Forbes.com

Chapter Seal:

- *Drive: The Surprising Truth About What Motivates* by Daniel H. Pink; Penguin Group (USA); Publication date: 4/5/2011

Chapter Urial:

- Steve Blank; *The Four Steps to the Epiphany*; K&S Ranch; 2nd edition (July 17, 2013)

  Chapter Xeme:

- http://www.cracked.com/article_18807_how-xerox-invented-information-age-and-gave-it-away.html

Chapter Yak:

- Karl Moore 2012] - Karl Moore, Contributor, Forbes.com; http://www.forbes.com/sites/karlmoore/2012/07/18/the-parachute-packer-the-best-story-i-have-ever-heard/; Karl Moore writes about how leadership must be rethought 7/18/2012

Chapter Zebra:

- Walter Isaacson -*Steve Jobs* ; Simon & Schuster; 1 edition (October 24, 2011)

Appendix A:

Tom Rath, *StrengthsFinder 2.0*; Gallup Press; NY, NY, 1st edition (February 1, 2007)

Dan Pink, "HOW TO CONDUCT AN AUTONOMY AUDIT", http://www.danpink.com/yamjam/YamJam; accessed 12/27/2013

D. Mitroff Silvers, M. Rogers and M. Wilson, Design Thinking for Visitor Engagement: Tackling One Museum's Big Challenge through Human-centered Design. In *Museums and the Web 2013*, N. Proctor & R. Cherry (eds). Silver Spring, MD: Museums and the Web. Published February 1, 2013. Consulted December 29, 2013; http://mw2013.museumsandtheweb.com/paper/design-thinking/

Eric Ries, *The Lean Startup, How Today's Entrepreneurs Use Continuous Innovation to Create Radically Successful Businesses,* Crown Publishing (September 13, 2011)

Harvard Business Review - "The Innovation Catalysts and Intuit"; HBR website: http://hbr.org/2011/06/the-innovation-catalysts/ar/1

www.ingramcontent.com/pod-product-compliance
Lightning Source LLC
Chambersburg PA
CBHW041829090426
42811CB00038B/2362/J